Lecture Notes in Business Information Processing   **418**

More information about this series at http://www.springer.com/series/7911

Aravinda Garimella · Prasanna Karhade ·
Abhishek Kathuria · Xiao Liu · Jennifer Xu ·
Kexin Zhao (Eds.)

The Role of e-Business during the Time of Grand Challenges

19th Workshop on e-Business, WeB 2020
Virtual Event, December 12, 2020
Revised Selected Papers

Springer

Editors
Aravinda Garimella 🅞
University of Illinois Urbana-Champaign
Champaign, IL, USA

Prasanna Karhade 🅞
University of Hawaii at Manoa
Honolulu, HI, USA

Abhishek Kathuria 🅞
Indian School of Business
Hyderabad, India

Xiao Liu 🅞
Arizona State University
Tempe, AZ, USA

Jennifer Xu 🅞
Bentley University
Waltham, MA, USA

Kexin Zhao 🅞
University of North Carolina at Charlotte
Charlotte, NC, USA

ISSN 1865-1348   ISSN 1865-1356 (electronic)
Lecture Notes in Business Information Processing
ISBN 978-3-030-79453-8   ISBN 978-3-030-79454-5 (eBook)
https://doi.org/10.1007/978-3-030-79454-5

This Springer imprint is published by the registered company Springer Nature Switzerland AG
The registered company address is: Gewerbestrasse 11, 6330 Cham, Switzerland

Preface

This book constitutes revised selected papers from the 19th Workshop on e-Business, WeB 2020, which took place virtually, on December 12, 2020.

The purpose of WeB is to provide a forum for researchers and practitioners to discuss findings, novel ideas, and lessons learned to address major challenges and map out the future directions for e-Business. The WeB 2020 theme was "**The Role of e-Business during the Time of Grand Challenges**."

We are facing many global economic, health, and development challenges nowadays, and information technologies and e-Business applications play a vital role in designing and implementing innovative solutions to address those challenges. Information technology has transformed business operations, fostered new business models and markets, enabled experts around the world to collaborate virtually, and provided financial inclusion to millions of unbanked populations in developing countries. For instance, in 2020, when the COVID-19 pandemic disrupted many aspects of lives, economies, and societies, digital technologies and e-Business models were leveraged to mitigate damages caused by the pandemic.

While technology has created many opportunities, limitations and frictions persist. Benefits created by technology innovations may not distribute fairly across socioeconomic classes or between developing and developed countries. Findings based on research conducted in WEIRD (western, educated, industrialized, rich and democratic) domains may not generalize to the rest of the world. Growing, rural, eastern, aspirational, transitional (GREAT) domains now account for a significant proportion of world economic output, thereby warranting special attention from information systems researchers. Digital inclusion is another issue, where some segments of our society do not have sufficient digital access or literacy to benefit from global digital networks. Therefore, we call for research that explores the role of e-Business during the time of grand challenges.

The 12 papers included in this volume were carefully reviewed and selected from a total of 24 submissions. The contributions are organized in topical sections as follows: Cybersecurity and COVID-19 challenges; digital platforms; and managing human factors in e-business.

December 2020

Aravinda Garimella
Prasanna Karhade
Abhishek Kathuria
Xiao Liu
Jennifer Xu
Kexin Zhao

Organization

Honorary Chairs

Andrew B. Whinston   University of Texas at Austin, USA
Hsinchun Chen   University of Arizona, USA

Conference Co-chairs

Michael J. Shaw   University of Illinois at Urbana-Champaign, USA
Bin Zhu   Oregon State University, USA
Han Zhang   Georgia Institute of Technology, USA
Kenny Cheng   University of Florida, USA
Ming Fan   University of Washington, USA
Karl Lang   City University of New York, USA

Program Organizing Co-chairs

Aravinda Garimella   University of Illinois at Urbana-Champaign, USA
Prasanna Karhade   University of Hawai'i at Mānoa, USA
Abhishek Kathuria   Indian School of Business, India
Xiao Liu   Arizona State University, USA
Jennifer Xu   Bentley University, USA
Kexin Zhao   University of North Carolina at Charlotte, USA

Program Committee

Hsin-lu Chang   National Chengchi University, Taiwan
Michael Chau   The University of Hong Kong, China
Cheng Chen   University of Wisconsin-Milwaukee, USA
Ching-chin Chern   National Taiwan University, Taiwan
Huihui Chi   ESCP Business School, France
Su Dong   Fayetteville State University, USA
Yuheng Hu   University of Illinois at Chicago, USA
Jinghua Huang   Tsinghua University, China
Seongmin Jeon   Gachon University, South Korea
Chunghan Kang   Seoul National University, South Korea
Dan Ke   Wuhan University, China
Sarah Khan   North Carolina State University, USA
Anthony Lee   National Taiwan University, Taiwan
Hsun-Ming Lee   Texas State University, USA

Shengli Li	Peking University, China
Chenwei Li	The University of Hong Kong, China
Xitong Li	HEC Paris, France
Jifeng Luo	Shanghai Jiaotong University, China
Selwyn Piramuthu	University of Florida, USA
Liangfei Qiu	University of Florida, USA
Raghu Santanam	Arizona State University, USA
Yufei Shen	HEC Paris, France
Riyaz Sikora	University of Texas at Arlington, USA
Vijayan Sugumaran	Oakland University, USA
James Thong	Hong Kong University of Science and Technology, China
Kai Wang	National University of Kaohsiung, Taiwan
Jason Xiong	Appalachian State University, USA
Lizhen Xu	Georgia Institute of Technology, USA
Dezhi Yin	University of South Florida, USA
Muhammad Adeel Zaffar	Lehore University of Management Sciences, Pakistan
Wei Zhang	University of Massachusetts at Boston, USA
Peiqin Zhang	Texas State University, USA
Wenqi Zhou	Duquesne University, USA
Wei Zhou	ESCP Business School, France

Contents

Cybersecurity and COVID-19 Challenges

The Next Global Financial Crisis Could Be Caused by Efforts to Prevent the Cyberattack

Keman Huang[1,2]([:envelope:]) [iD] and Stuart Madnick[2] [iD]

[1] Renmin University of China, Beijing 100086, China
keman@ruc.edu.cn
[2] Cybersecurity at MIT Sloan, MIT, Cambridge, MA 02142, USA
smadnick@mit.edu

Abstract. In the era of Web-based services and Internet-of-Things (IoT), almost every product and service is Internet-connected. Providers want their products and services to capture data, in part to improve performance and consumer satisfaction, but these might also be tools for spying and other malicious activities. Hence cybersecurity has increasingly been invoked from the perspective of "national security," directly impacting international trade and investment policy. The press has largely focused on trade issues between the USA and China, especially regarding Huawei. However, the scope of such cybersecurity impacts goes far beyond these two countries. As part of our research investigation, we identified and analyzed 33 cases, which involved 19 countries. So this is a truly global phenomenon that needs to be addressed. This paper presents a taxonomy developed to understand the different circumstances, actions, and outcomes.

Keywords: Cybersecurity · International trade · Trade restrictions · Financial crisis · Cyberattack

1 Introduction and Motivation

There have been headlines like "A cyberattack could trigger the next financial crisis" [1] and "How a Cyberattack Could Cause the Next Financial Crisis." [2] These should be of concern to all of us and be important incentives to do something. But what should be done? As we explain in this paper, actions taken to prevent such a cyberattack may, in fact, be the actual cause of a major financial crisis – even a global international trade crisis.

Issues of international trade policy have gained increased attention. Of course, restrictions on international trade regarding technology have long existed – on imports and exports, as well as on direct foreign investment. But cybersecurity has not been a key issue for trade policy – until now.

In the era of Web-based services and Internet-of-Things (IoT), almost every product and service is Internet-connected. Manufacturers want their products and services to capture data, in part to improve performance and consumer satisfaction, but these might

A. Garimella et al. (Eds.): WeB 2020, LNBIP 418, pp. 3–11, 2021.
https://doi.org/10.1007/978-3-030-79454-5_1

also be tools for spying and other malicious activities. Hence cybersecurity has increasingly been invoked from the perspective of "national security," with a direct impact on international trade and investment policy [3–6].

Furthermore, data is considered a critical asset that supports digital service industries with increasing concern about data sovereignty [7]. As a result, it is not just products that would be impacted, but also services, such as international banking and payment systems [8]. We have recently seen effects to restrict or ban web services such as TikTok and WeChat [19].

From a defensive perspective, since it is impossible to thoroughly examine the millions of lines of software or firmware in these products, what should countries do to prevent cyber intrusions when these products can introduce cyber attack vectors? One approach that has been often suggested and increasingly implemented is excluding any potentially dangerous products or services coming from questionable countries. But this raises important policy issues, such as (1) what is a dangerous product or service and (2) what a questionable country is? Assuming such restrictions quickly become worldwide policies with retaliations, what might be the ultimate impact on international trade and the economy? Possibly a major financial crisis.

As an effort to explore ways to maintain an open and cyber secure international trade system and avoid the above dilemma, this paper aims to understand the current landscape of how countries and companies manage cybersecurity issues within the digital trade system. Based on the 33 cases we identified, our preliminary results demonstrate that such cybersecurity is an increasing global governance issue. The diverse actions and outcomes highlight the essential requirement to construct a global governance framework to avoid a recurrence of the "Smoot-Hawley Tariff" disaster within the digital age.

2   Literature Review: Cybersecurity Within Digital Trade

Cross-border data flows play a critical role in digital trade. Most studies about the linkage between digital trade and restrictive policies focus on data restriction policies, such as data localization or privacy regulations [20]. For example, increasingly regarding Artificial Intelligence (AI), trade policies related to privacy, data localization, privileged access to government data, industrial regulation related to standards and source code, can have a negative impact on international trade [21]. However, the digital trade policies due to cybersecurity concern are much broader than just the data restriction policies [22] and include policies related to tariffs on digital goods, filtering and blocking, Intellectual Property Rights (IPR) infringement, national standards, and burdensome conformity assessment and regulations to limit disinformation, etc.

On the other hand, the reterritorialization of cyberspace as a national cyber territory has become a reality [7], and many nations have expanded or are expanding their authority into cyberspace. Many studies discuss cybersecurity within digital trade from the international relation context and explore how cybersecurity changes international governance [23, 24]. We are also witnessing cybersecurity concerns regarding digital trade reshaping the international business environment, and international corporations need to understand the associated risks [9]. However, the interactions and outcomes are highly diverse due to the dynamics among countries (both host and home countries) and corporations (both domestic and international enterprises).

This study aims to unfold the phenomenon around cybersecurity governance within digital trade and create an overview framework to explore the different implementations of policies and the dynamics among countries and corporations.

3   Methodology

As part of our research investigation [9], we used "cybersecurity" and "international trade/digital trade" as the keywords to search the news. Then we went through the relevant news and only considered those cases that involved at least two countries. For each case, we further collected publicly reported interactions among those countries and companies to grasp the dynamics within each case. For example, for the Huawei case in the USA, we can trace back to 2008. Digesting these cases enables us to develop a preliminary framework, focusing on the different actions that countries and corporations took. We further hosted workshop discussions with senior executives, managers, and researchers from Fortune 500 companies, and cybersecurity solution providers who are industrial members of our consortium, Cybersecurity at MIT Sloan (CAMS), to discuss these cases and identify additional cases. We repeat this process to add cases and verify the developed framework.

Through this process, we identified at least 33 cases, which involved 19 countries, and developed the framework we reported in the following sections. Note that in this study, we don't intend to develop a comprehensive case library but focus on the coverage of the diverse countries, products/services, actions, and outcomes.

4   A Glance on the Increasing Scope of Impact

The press has largely focused on trade issues between the USA and China, especially regarding Huawei and now TikTok and WeChat. But the scope of such cybersecurity impacts goes far beyond these two countries. As shown in Fig. 1, the 33 cases we identified have involved 19 countries.

Fig. 1. Countries that instituted international trade restrictions due to cybersecurity concerns

When these cases are studied, a complex web of impacts quickly becomes clear, as shown in Fig. 2. The point is that, even at this rather early stage, this is already a worldwide phenomenon and growing. In Fig. 2, the direction indicates the source nation to impacted nations (note: many go in both directions), and the number indicates the number of occurrences in our collection of 33 cases.

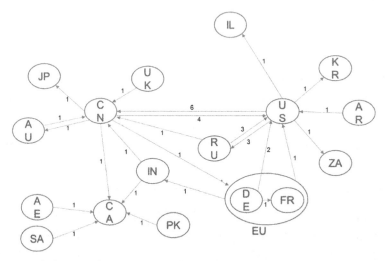

Fig. 2. Network diagram of ccountries with international trade restrictions due to cybersecurity concerns

As just one example regarding the voice-activated 'My Friend, Cayla' doll, made in the U.S., there was a concern that potentially it could spy on children or anyone in the room, collecting personal data, so "On 17 February 2017, Germany banned both the sale and ownership … alleging that it contains a concealed surveillance device' that violates federal privacy regulations." [10] There are many other such cases. Increasing prohibitions on the import or export of products and services could certainly have an impact on international trade and world economies. But, there can also be even more direct impacts. Currently, there are over one quadrillion dollars, that is 1000 trillion, a year of cross-border monetary payments. Consider this real headline, "Amazon sellers get caught in US-China trade spat as money transfer service abruptly closes." [11] What caused the problem? The answer was that "U.S. blocks MoneyGram sale to China's Ant Financial on national security concerns." [12].

5 Framework for Studying Cybersecurity Impact on International Trade

We have developed a framework, shown in Fig. 3, to systematically organize the details of each of the cases identified, especially the timeline, related actors, actions, and impacts for each case. This framework focuses on demonstrating the dynamics of the cybersecurity impact on international trade and addresses not only compliance issues, but also the business and geopolitical issues.

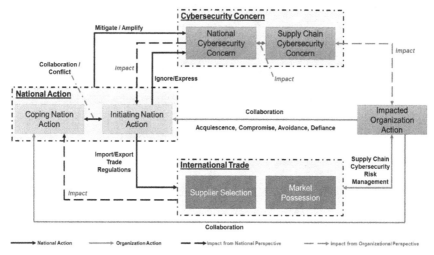

Fig. 3. Framework for the impact on cybersecurity concern on international trade

Scope of National Cyber Security Concerns. The definition of national cyber security is often intentionally vague to achieve some operating space [13], but there is no doubt that national cyber security is a multi-dimensional concept, and all the different perspectives must be considered, including military security, political security, economic security, and culture security. Most organizations, not only businesses but also governments, are becoming increasingly reliant on global supply chains, including both digital and physical supply chains. The most famous example using the supply chain vulnerability was the Stuxnet attack on the Iran nuclear enrichment facility. It was allegedly accomplished by planting malware in the industrial control system, which was then shipped to Iran, resulting in the destruction of many centrifuges [14]. Note that national cybersecurity and supply chain cybersecurity are not isolated. For example, the U.S. Department of Defense (DoD) "buys products from international commercial and mixed defense and non-defense companies that service many customers, both within and outside of defense markets" [15].

Hence, the cybersecurity of the supply chain for critical infrastructures will raise concerns about the nation's cybersecurity. On the other hand, the concerns of national cybersecurity impact the perception about the risks from supply chains and further impact the business' concerns on the supply chain cybersecurity.

Different Actions and Dynamic Outcomes Possible. There are many different circumstances, leading to different actions and outcomes. Using the framework above, the actors, actions, and impacts for each of the 33 cases studied are studied and reported in [16]. Figure 4 gives a high-level summary, the 33 cases are across the horizontal, and the differing circumstances, actions, and outcomes are along the vertical. A checkmark with a yellow marker is shown whenever the circumstances, actions, and outcomes apply. The critical thing to note is that even with this relatively small sample of cases, there is a wide variety of cases and actions. The reader is referred to [16] for the details.

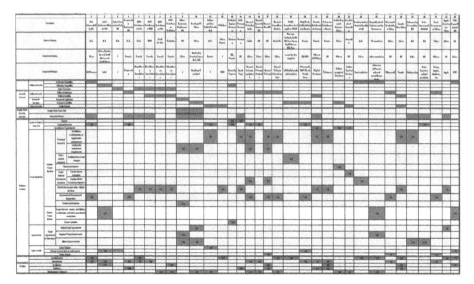

Fig. 4. Matrix listing the cases studied and their differing circumstances, actions, outcomes

To illustrate some of the diversity, we will briefly discuss just two cases with different outcomes. These are cases involving Huawei in the U.S. and U.K. as examples of different actions and outcomes.

In 2011, worried about potential spying, the U.S. government blocked a bid from Huawei to help build a new national wireless network for first responders such as police, firefighters, and ambulances. In 2012, the U.S. further released a report urging U.S. telecommunication companies not to do business with Huawei Technologies Co Ltd and ZTE Corp because it said potential Chinese state influence on the companies posed a threat to U.S. security. In 2013, Washington ordered several major government departments, including NASA and the Justice and Commerce Departments, to seek approval from federal law enforcement officials before purchasing I.T. equipment from all Chinese vendors, requiring the agencies to make a formal assessment of "cyber-espionage or sabotage" risk in consultation with law enforcement authorities when considering buying information technology systems. Finally, in 2014, Huawei decided to exit the U.S. market largely.

On the other hand, in 2010, Huawei opened its Cyber Security Evaluation Centre in the U.K. "The new Cyber Security Evaluation Centre is a key part of Huawei's end-to-end global security assurance system. This center is like a glasshouse – transparent, readily accessible, and open to regulators and our customers." [17] In 2013, when the parliamentary intelligence and security committee (ISC) raised concerns that Huawei's equipment could be used by Beijing to spy on the U.K., and called for an urgent inquiry, the U.K. National Security Adviser published the executive summary to the ISC on a review of Huawei's Cyber Security Evaluation Centre (HCSEC), concluding that "The review judged that the HCSEC was operating effectively and achieving its objectives". In early 2014, Huawei Cyber Security Evaluation Centre (HCSEC) Oversight Board, was further established on the recommendation of the U.K. National Security Adviser to oversee and ensure the independence, competence, and overall effectiveness of HCSEC. Every year it releases a report about any risks to U.K. national security from Huawei's involvement in the U.K.'s critical networks and makes sure that these risks have been sufficiently mitigated.

Hence, though the U.S. continues to lock Huawei out from its 5G market, on 28 January 2020, it was reported that "U.K. government approves Huawei 5G deal." [18]. Note that due to the dynamic political environment between the USA, China, and the U.K., on July 14, 2020, the U.K.'s decision is changed again, requiring telecom operators not to buy any new equipment from Huawei after the end of 2020 and remove Huawei equipment by 2027.

6   Example from the Past: Smoot-Hawley Tariff

Let us now look to the past to see how there could be a major breakdown of international trade, and how that could create a global financial crisis. In the aftermath of the stock market crash of October 1929 and the following impacts on the economy, the U.S. Congress enacted the United States Tariff Act of 1930, commonly referred to as the Smoot-Hawley Tariff. It increased tariffs on foreign imports to the U.S. by about 20% on top of already high import duties on foreign agricultural products and manufactured goods. But what were the consequences? At least 25 countries responded by increasing their own tariffs on American goods. As a result, global trade plummeted, in the USA there was a reduction of exports and imports by 67%, contributing to the ill effects on the world economy. In essence, it made the Great Depression much greater!

This mishap was finally reversed, starting with the Reciprocal Trade Agreements Act of 1934. But, the increasing use of international trade barriers and restrictions discussed earlier, followed by retaliations, could produce a similar chain of events. It would be good not to see history repeated.

7   Conclusion

With the increasing development of and dependence on the digital economy, cyberspace plays a critical role in international trade. We have found many ways that cybersecurity concerns can impact international trade. As part of our research investigation, we identified and analyzed 33 cases, which involved 19 countries. So this is truly a global phenomenon that needs to be addressed.

Due to the lack of consensus on cyberspace behavior norms and the vague definitions of national cyber security, we can expect even more cyber conflicts and their negative impact on international trade.

However, instead of each nation proposing its own set of norms that will inevitably be at odds with one other, finding common ground and working together to construct cyber norms is an important task.

Also, instead of only considering cybersecurity a regulation issue and trying to comply with the emerging regulations, companies should become actively involved in the regulation processes, not only during the comment periods but also during the regulation draft process. With a cool mind and careful academic study, effective norms can be developed, and the worse case scenarios can be avoided.

Acknowledgment. This research was supported, in part, by funds from the members of the Cybersecurity at MIT Sloan (CAMS) consortium.

References

1. Pisani, B.: A cyberattack could trigger the next financial crisis, new report says. CNBC (2018). https://www.cnbc.com/2018/09/13/a-cyberattack-could-trigger-the-next-financial-crisis.html
2. Mee, P., Schuermann, T.: How a cyber attack could cause the next financial crisis. Harvard Business Review (2018). https://hbr.org/2018/09/how-a-cyber-attack-could-cause-the-next-financial-crisis
3. Friedman, A.A.: Cybersecurity and Trade: National Policies, Global and Local Consequences. Brookings Institution Center for Technology Innovation (September), pp. 1–18 (2013)
4. Kshetri, N.: Cybersecurity-Related Barriers to International Trade and Investment. The Quest to Cyber Superiority (2016). http://papers.ssrn.com/sol3/papers.cfm?abstract_id=2809819
5. Mata, D.C.: Cybersecurity dimensions of national security. J. Law Admin. Sci., 132–142 (2015)
6. Farrell, H., Newman, A.L.: Choke Points. Harvard Business Review, February 2020
7. Lambach, D.: The Territorialization of Cyberspace. Int. Stud. Rev. **22**, 1–25 (2019). https://doi.org/10.1093/isr/viz022
8. Huang, K., Madnick, S.E.: Cyber securing cross-border financial services: calling for a financial cybersecurity action task force. In: 19th Annual Security Conference, pp. 1–10 (2020). https://doi.org/10.2139/ssrn.3544325
9. Madnick, S., Johnson, S., Huang, K.: What Countries and Companies Can Do When Trade and Cybersecurity Overlap. Harvard Business Review, 1–6 January 2019
10. Emery, D.: 'My Friend Cayla' Doll Records Children's Speech, Is Vulnerable to Hackers (2017). https://www.snopes.com/news/2017/02/24/my-friend-cayla-doll-privacy-concerns/
11. Levy, A.: Amazon sellers get caught in US-China trade spat as money transfer service abruptly closes (2019). https://www.cnbc.com/2019/02/01/worldfirst-abruptly-closes-us-operations-amid-ant-financial-deal-talks.html
12. Roumeliotis, G.: U.S. Blocks MoneyGram sale to China's Ant Financial on national security concerns (2018). https://www.reuters.com/article/us-moneygram-intl-m-a-ant-financial/u-s-blocks-moneygram-sale-to-chinas-ant-financial-on-national-security-concerns-idUSKBN1ER1R7
13. Lockett, J.: Where High and Low Politics Meet: National Security and Cybersecurity. World Economic Forum, 18–21 August 2015
14. Clayton, M.: Exclusive: New thesis on how Stuxnet infiltrated Iran nuclear facility (2014). https://www.csmonitor.com/World/Security-Watch/2014/0225/Exclusive-New-thesis-on-how-Stuxnet-infiltrated-Iran-nuclear-facility
15. Gansler, J.S., Lucyshyn, W., Harrington, L.H.: Defense Supply Chain Security: Current State and Opportunities for Improvement (2012)
16. Huang, K., Madnick, S.E., Johnson, S.: Interactions between cybersecurity and international trade: a systematic framework. SSRN Electr. J. (2018). http://web.mit.edu/smadnick/www/wp/2018-13.pdf
17. Reichert, C.: U.K. cybersecurity agency finds new low-risk concerns with Huawei's security centre (2018). https://www.zdnet.com/article/uk-cybersecurity-agency-finds-new-low-risk-concerns-with-huaweis-security-centre/

18. Vaughan, A.: U.K. government approves Huawei 5G deal despite security fears (2020). https://www.newscientist.com/article/2231678-uk-government-approves-huawei-5g-deal-despite-security-fears/#ixzz6RAbCtYgb
19. Huang, K., Madnick, S.E.: The TikTok Ban Should Worry Every Company, Harvard Business Review, 28 August 2020
20. Ferracane, M., Kren, J., van der Marel, E.: Do data policy restrictions impact the productivity performance of firms and industries? SSRN Electr. J. (2019)
21. Agrawal, A., Gans, J., Goldfarb, A.: A.I. and international trade. In: The Economics of Artificial Intelligence, pp. 463–492 (2019)
22. Aaronson, S.A.: What are we talking about when we discuss digital protectionism? In SSRN (2018). https://doi.org/10.2139/ssrn.3032108
23. Carr, M.: Public – private partnerships in national cyber-security strategies. Int. Aff. **92**(1), 43–62 (2016)
24. Xuetong, Y.: Bipolar rivalry in the early digital age. Chinese J. Int. Politics **13**(3), 313–341 (2020)

Tackling Cybersecurity Regulatory Challenges: A Proposed Research Framework

Angelica Marotta[1]([⊠]) [iD] and Stuart Madnick[2] [iD]

[1] MIT Sloan School of Management, 245 First Street, Cambridge, MA 02142, USA
amarotta@mit.edu
[2] MIT Sloan School of Management, 100 Main Street, Cambridge, MA 02142, USA
smadnick@mit.edu

Abstract. Although concerns about cybersecurity have been around for more than a decade with significant attention by governments and regulators, the problem has actually continued to increase. So, it is clear that whatever is being done is not working. The research question for this study is: To what extent does compliance help or hinder cybersecurity for the organization – and why/how. When trying to understand the interplay between compliance and cybersecurity, generally, two scenarios may occur: (1) compliance helps security or (2) compliance hinders security – or maybe both. This research attempts to provide a better understanding of the factors by evaluating compliance as a critical factor in the organization's cybersecurity strategy through a series of corporate and government interviews to affirm, refute, and refine our initial hypotheses.

Keywords: Cybersecurity · Compliance · Regulations · Maturity level · Country culture

1 Introduction

Today, in order to be successful, every organization needs to be cyber secure. Cybersecurity is the practice of protecting the confidentiality, integrity, and availability of critical organizational assets. However, this practice can be complex and time-consuming, and typically is not the primary strategic goal for the majority of organizations. Conversely, compliance is one of the most powerful motivating forces behind most business investments due to the financial or reputational impact it may have. Compliance is generally defined as the act of conforming to rules or policies. In most industries, ensuring the application of these rules or policies often means meeting a third party's regulatory requirements, such as a government or a cybersecurity framework. Nevertheless, meeting compliance regulations doesn't necessarily enable an organization to cover all cybersecurity needs. This means that achieving the highest level in compliance does not always mean that is also possible to achieve an equally high level in cybersecurity.

The research question for this study is: To what extent does compliance help or hinder security for the organization – and why/how. In particular, this research question aims to identify the indicators contributing to a higher or lower synergy between cybersecurity

© Springer Nature Switzerland AG 2021
A. Garimella et al. (Eds.): WeB 2020, LNBIP 418, pp. 12–24, 2021.
https://doi.org/10.1007/978-3-030-79454-5_2

and compliance. Cybersecurity compliance is not only about having documented procedures; it is also about the positive or negative impact a compliance program can have on an organizational cybersecurity posture. In this paper, we will discuss why compliance is a key concern – from the needs facing businesses with different levels of maturity and industries to the difficulties of operating in diverse cultural and geographical contexts. In this paper, firstly, we will examine the possible scenarios of compliance successes and failures through a theoretical and practical review of the literature. Secondly, we will consider hypotheses concerning the causes of the examined situations. Finally, we will propose a methodology for addressing the research question.

2 Literature Review and Background

In recent years, regulatory compliance has emerged as a "grey area," which is trying to find its position in the evolving cybersecurity landscape. Previous studies on compliance have highlighted several important issues concerning compliance in cybersecurity. Most of them involved problems deriving from incorrect management of behavioral compliance (i.e., adjusting a group or an organization's values, beliefs, and behavior patterns toward the desired compliance outcomes) [2, 3, 12, 20, 25, 30]. Attitude towards compliance with cybersecurity regulations may have a significant impact on decision-making regarding cybersecurity choices. However, while behavioral studies in this field have expanded the understanding of regulatory compliance from various perspectives, other areas need to be addressed. Examples include, but are not limited to, the evolution of regulations, regulatory responsibilities, regulation language, etc. In this regard, an emerging research stream on the topic focuses on the growing need to move from the traditional view of compliance as a management subject to a more complex phenomenon [6]. For example [14] argues that the current literature is still at an early stage in terms of explaining the disconnect between security and compliance. In this paper, the authors highlight the importance of integrating the current research on security with additional research into security compliance. Following this trend, our research focuses on filling the current gaps through an empirical approach to examine different compliance situations. Therefore, when trying to understand the interplay between compliance and cybersecurity, generally, two scenarios may occur:

Compliance Helps Security. Although compliance doesn't always equal security, in some cases, it can help increase security [27]. For instance, in Germany, a hacker stole unencrypted data on hundreds of thousands of customers of a company because the company had failed to implement adequate security measures under the General Data Protection Regulation (GDPR) [28]. As a result, the company received a € 20,000 fine for failing to follow fundamental security practices and then adopted the needed procedures to avoid future fines. Therefore, even though, compliance requirements often offer the bare minimum in terms of security protocols, for some companies the existence of regulations may cause them to at least achieve the overall goal of a basic cybersecurity posture. This has also been observed in a 2017 online survey conducted by Texas-based company SolarWinds, which interviewed around 200 federal government IT decision makers and influencers [21]. The purpose of this survey was to determine the challenges faced by IT professionals to prevent security threats. Results revealed that sixty-eight percent of respondents agreed that the implementation of relevant standards was critical to achieving their cybersecurity targets and sixty percent agreed that compliance has helped them improve their agency's cybersecurity capabilities. Therefore, in some cases, meeting compliance requires companies to reconsider their procedures and address critical gaps. If a company is motivated to worry about fulfilling compliance requirements, which also include cybersecurity, it is likely that the company is also more motivated to allocate additional resources and create favorable conditions for better cybersecurity than a company that is not focused on compliance.

Another positive aspect of being compliant is that regulations may help companies hold their teams accountable to actually implementing the necessary practices, making it difficult for attackers to breach their systems or cause irreparable damages. For example, a Report of Cybersecurity Practices by the Financial Industry Regulatory Authority (FINRA) tells the story of how one of its reviewed firms interpreted FINRA obligations to respond to a cyber-attack through the concept of accountability [24]. One of the firm's first steps, for instance, was establishing a leader for the incident response process and an internal leader for each type of incident as well. Additionally, they identified the role of every person involved in the process and the workflow of the response steps. This approach helped the company repair some of the reputational damage caused by an attack and keep its employees accountable for their actions.

Compliance Hinders Security. A company may have managed to implement the controls outlined in a specific regulation, which describes the necessary requirements to protect its data [16] however, that does not mean that its network and systems are still completely protected from cyber threats or that an employee will not send sensitive data via email by mistake. The process of achieving compliance is often costly and exhausting. Additionally, since organizations employ different structures for the management of compliance and cybersecurity there may be conflicts of interests between different entities or units. Therefore, it's not unusual for organizations to let compliance be a substitute for their cybersecurity strategy, considering the amount of time, money, and effort involved in implementing compliance activities. Regardless of whether a company demonstrates a low or a high level of compliance, the compliance processes are generally the same and often involve predefined protocols based on checklists and spreadsheet questions. However, the "checklist mindset", while good for gap analysis, may turn into one of the major risks to be addressed in a developed organizational environment. Consequently, even though companies meet regulation requirements, they may still experience major attacks. For example, despite being within the scope of PCI DSS compliance, Equifax suffered a data breach that impacted over 143 million customers [19].

In this case, compliance did not eliminate the probability of breaches. In recent years, many organizations that suffered major data breaches have claimed their systems were violated despite being fully PCI compliant. For example, Target, a U.S. company operating in the retail sector, suffered from a data breach that exposed credit and debit card data on more than 100 million customers [10]. Just like Equifax, the company was PCI compliant at the time of the attack. This is particularly relevant when considering that regulatory requirements become outdated quickly in the cybersecurity sector or may be misinterpreted. This may increase the risk of data breaches by forcing companies to adhere to obsolete or unclear cybersecurity requirements. Furthermore, being "in compliance" may produce a false sense of security – making the organization even more vulnerable. For example, MEDantex, a Kansas-based healthcare company, leaked sensitive patient medical records despite, apparently, claiming to be HIPAA compliant, as they had announced on their website [15, 31]:

> *"MEDantex is serious about keeping your data secure. We are HIPAA-compliant, and our servers are protected with 128-bit encryption. Our security and HIPAA compliance team is made up of department managers and headed by a security officer that continually monitors your data."*

HIPAA defines a large set of rules and procedures, many of which require proper technology that provides the security features suggested by HIPAA guidelines. However, like other regulations, these regulation guidelines are open to interpretation, leaving it up to employees to determine the best way to fulfill the requirements. In the healthcare industry, there may be a number of risks associated with misinterpretation because most of the employees who work for a healthcare organization may be specialized in patient care but may not necessarily have the technical skills to correctly manage a compliant cybersecurity infrastructure. As a result, this may cause costly mistakes and show people that there is a lack of care when securing medical information.

This example also shows that the relationship between compliance and cybersecurity can also become more complicated when the privacy component is involved. The concept of privacy has evolved with the introduction of information technologies - from "the right to be let alone" as Samuel D. Warren and Louis D. Brandeis formulated, now privacy mainly refers to the right to access and control the use and circulation of personal data through digital channels [11]. Therefore, in today's digital environment, although the issue of privacy is crucial, it is data privacy that is of primary importance rather than privacy per se. Data privacy is generally focused on the proper governance of data. This generally involves implementing regulation requirements to ensure that individuals' personal data are only being collected, used, shared, and transferred in appropriate ways. In this context, cybersecurity plays a key role in building privacy as it helps to protect data from unauthorized access and prevent data breaches. However, even though cybersecurity, privacy, and compliance are all connected, the three can sometimes be in conflict. Often, these issues arise when making decisions about how to manage data. Some regulations, for example, may require organizations to adopt solutions with which cybersecurity is aligned but privacy is not. The conflicting interplay may also work the other way around - compliance can complicate cybersecurity when certain laws or regulations impose privacy measures that interfere with or limit the access to information, which would be useful to guarantee security (e.g. if privacy requirements hinder the use of protection solutions aimed at countering data leaks). In most cases, these types of issues arise when the application of privacy requirements guarantees individuals' right to privacy while preventing authorities from collecting important information to conduct investigations. For example, tracking down a suspect of a crime may be useful to solve a criminal case, but, at the same time, this may violate the alleged criminal's privacy or some aspects of privacy.

The framework resulting from these scenarios is an overall organizational situation in which compliance can be either an excellent starting point to develop the appropriate cybersecurity culture within an organization or an obstacle that will only lead an organization to a false sense of security. However, often, whether compliance is a positive or negative factor in achieving cybersecurity is not black and white but rather a matter of a series of factors, which may either minimize or maximize the impact of compliance on cybersecurity. This research attempts to provide a better understanding of these factors by evaluating compliance as a critical factor in the organization's cybersecurity strategy.

3 Proposed Research

This study is proposed with the purpose of providing an analysis of the role of compliance in affecting or facilitating the achievement of cybersecurity. The main hypothesis of this research project is that the extent to which compliance is effective depends on three factors: an organization's cybersecurity maturity level, the cultural differences between countries, and the industry segment organizations operate in.

H1. Maturity Level

a. If an organization has achieved compliance, it might neglect important aspects of security that have not been addressed – putting itself at risk.

One of the main goals of regulations is ensuring that organizations reach and maintain a specified level of preparedness and capacity for meeting certain objectives about cybersecurity (i.e., cybersecurity maturity level). If an organization is, for example, mature enough to sustain the level required by regulations, it will probably only focus on complying with the required security standards and will not be motivated to implement additional cybersecurity policies and processes.

b. If an organization is very weak in security, regulations might guide and force the organization to improve.

Organizations with lower levels of maturity may view compliance as a motivating factor in achieving better cybersecurity and staying vigilant in their cybersecurity operations [29]. For example, in the case study "A Culture of Cybersecurity at Banca Popolare di Sondrio," Banca Popolare di Sondrio (BPS) built its success on its ability to leverage the power of technology to provide better and more secure services for its customers [17]. When the Bank started its digital transformation, its practices and processes were not mature enough to sustain the continuous cybersecurity readiness of the whole system. However, being an organization operating in a highly regulated environment, the implementation of regulations positively impacted various aspects within the Bank and helped it move towards a more proactive maturity level. The introduction of GDPR particularly forced employees to change their cybersecurity habits. For example, employees started to follow established cybersecurity practices and implement new organizational measures to ensure an appropriate level of cybersecurity to prevent data breaches.

c. An organization may think (or even "stretch things") so as to appear compliant (and secure) to save costs – without much actual regard to security.

The cost of being compliant can sometimes be a burden for organizations that are not cyber mature. It requires a lot of paperwork to manage, and it needs to be handled correctly since an error or omission can lead to consequences, such as legal actions, penalties, and sometimes, loss of the requirements to operate or do business in a given industry. This could result in organizations being under pressure, therefore neglecting or completely ignoring security measures. For this reason, they often check the compliance "checkbox" and do the least about security just to pass audits. This is a common approach but unfortunately, it prevents organizations from having the means to reflect on the impact that regulations may have on security. For example, some standards have different levels of compliance; each of them has specific requirements necessary to validate its compliance. In these cases, one of the largest problems is that organizations tend to have minimalistic approaches to meeting requirements because of the granularity of the compliance process. The family of PCI DSS standards, for instance, falls under this category of standards as it comprehends four levels of PCI compliance. One of the first cybersecurity requirements is to protect cardholder data by installing and maintaining a firewall configuration [23]. Although meeting this requirement seems to be sufficient from an audit perspective, given the vagueness about the degree to which this firewall must protect cardholder data, from a cybersecurity point of view, it may be necessary to implement additional measures. Thus, some organizations don't consider supplementary cybersecurity protections when they are not technically required.

Additionally, if meeting compliance requires organizations to make extra financial efforts in terms of security, they may decide to dedicate more time to appearing compliant and avoiding fines rather than actually ensuring compliance applicability. According to Javvad Malik, an IT security professional [22],

> "Organizations with small and overstretched security teams and limited budgets for cybersecurity are likely to be extremely worried about the threat of GDPR fines. After all, the potential of having to pay up to 4% of global turnover could have a serious effect on a fledgling business potentially impacting earnings or funding opportunities. They could also lose customers through reputational damage and even have to consider making redundancies. Set against this backdrop, it's easy to see why some might consider trying to cover up a data breach, rather than deal with the consequences. But this could lead to far greater problems for them in the long term."

This means that many organizations may decide to give up on security to prevent any issue associated with compliance penalties and hide their maturity "insecurities." For example, Article 33 of the GDPR introduces a duty on all organizations to report a data breach within 72 h. In order to avoid large fines, organizations might try to cover up data breaches rather than reporting them within 72 h. One reason for this could be a lack of preparation or adequate tools in identifying or reporting data breaches in a timely manner.

H2. Cultural Differences Between Countries

a. Compliance may have a negative or positive impact on the cybersecurity posture of an organization, depending on the cultural context in which it operates.

Regulations, especially those related to privacy, might vary greatly from one country to another. Consequently, some cybersecurity practices, for instance, may represent a problem in one country while, in other countries, the same practices would be considered correct. For example, the philosophy behind GDPR is that privacy is a fundamental right under the Charter of Fundamental Rights of the European Union [7]. Therefore, the new regulation is shaped around this principle and is intended to harmonize the way that personal data are processed throughout the EU.

In the United States, data protection is based on concepts of autonomy and liberty articulated in the US Constitution and the Bill of Rights and follows a more sectoral approach, according to which data protection is regulated depending on the category into which individuals' information falls [5]. Examples of this approach include the Gramm-Leach-Bliley Act (GLBA), which regulates financial services and the Health Insurance Portability and Accountability Act (HIPAA) which covers health data. This aspect can be especially important for multinational companies; considering the cultural differences of every country, it may be hard for them to achieve compliance through a unique strategy for every branch, and this may leave their organization exposed to potential vulnerabilities.

b. Compliance rules in different countries might be directly or indirectly in conflict.

Because of the global nature of cybersecurity, there may be a potential for conflicts when regulations differ across countries or cannot be applied beyond the boundaries of a specific country. This may create privacy and security concerns and may affect the sense of security. For example, it is worth mentioning the battle between Brazilian investigation authorities and U.S. companies [26]. One of the main issues behind this conflict lies in the fact that companies with headquarters in the U.S. that provide internet application services in Brazil face issues regarding the application of the Brazilian laws, especially when it comes to disclosing contents of users' communications stored in their servers to local law enforcement. In a case involving Microsoft, the Brazilian government requested the company to disclose email communications of an individual involved in a criminal investigation [1]. However, according to U.S. privacy laws, it is illegal to hand over the data stored in the U.S. even if they belong to a Brazilian citizen. Thus, Microsoft refused to fulfill the request and, as a result, a Brazilian Microsoft executive was arrested.

In Europe, one of the recent concerns involving cross-national compliance issues is the possible impact that Brexit may have on the rules around data security. According to a survey of over 900 participants, over a quarter of survey respondents believed that the corporate and customer data their organization holds would be less secure if Brexit happened [13]. If the UK were to leave the EU, the integration of GDPR into UK law could no longer be adequate to ensure that UK data security and privacy standards are accepted by the EU [9]. Therefore, without a new agreement, data flows between the UK and the EU would probably be affected, causing organizations to be more exposed to data breaches.

H3. Industry Segmentation and Different Regulators

a. Industry segmentation may affect a company's ability to build consistent cybersecurity strategies as they relate to regulations.

In addition to the geographical factor, regulations often vary according to the industry segment in which companies operate. For example, managing the financial sector represent a significant challenge for many companies because regulations within this type of industry vary significantly based on the type of financial service. Each of these regulations is aimed at establishing a set of robust cybersecurity practices, protecting costumers, and supporting the stability of the global economy [4]. However, due to the numerous requirements and the effort required to meet them, companies struggle to build consistent cybersecurity strategies.

For example, in a survey of chief information security officers from financial institutions, participants indicated that 40% of their team's time and resources were devoted to reconciling various regulatory requirements [8]. In most cases, regulations used differing vocabularies and lexicons to define the same cybersecurity concepts and practices, causing a significant burden for companies. In the financial field, this is particularly important as companies must demonstrate their compliance with the words mentioned in every single regulation. Additionally, there are different regulatory agencies and entities involved, such as the U.S. Treasury, the Financial Industry Regulatory Authority (FINRA), etc. Typically, the number of regulators that companies need to communicate with may vary from 2 (for small financial services) to 20 or more (for large organizations).

b. Regulators are often unprepared to address the rapidly changing cybersecurity landscape and have an adversarial, rather than collaborative, relationship with the companies being regulated.

In some heavily regulated industries, such as electric utilities, historically regulators were political appointees whose primary concerns were pricing policies – since the government was basically allowing these companies to operate as monopolies. Technical issues, especially new ones such as cybersecurity, were not usually in the backgrounds of most of these regulators.

Furthermore, regulators play a key role in the compliance process as they normally require companies to conduct assessments according to the framework they establish, and the results derived from these assessments need to be supported by documentary evidence. Therefore, this complicated regulatory environment may result in substantial financial impacts for organizations in terms of time, inefficiencies, and budget.

Although the goals of these regulations are usually to encourage "good behavior" by the companies, the actual impact could be quite different. In our interviews and studies, it was clear that in many cases, the regulatory process was treated as a "game." That is, the game was to pass the assessment audits with as little effort and cost as possible – without any serious concern about improving cybersecurity. In one case that we studied in the financial services industry, a prominent Asian bank operated as follows: in the short-time before the annual audit was to be conducted, significant effort was expended to get everything in order to pass the audit. As soon as the audit was completed and successfully passed, all those efforts were quickly abandoned. This process continued for many years, until it was hit with a serious cyberattack shortly after having passed its audit.

These hypotheses will serve as a guide to the design of the most appropriate research methodology and will be used to identify what data to collect. These hypotheses will then be evaluated with the aim to achieve a more detailed knowledge base around the influence of compliance on security.

4   Methodology

We propose to conduct this research in five stages. We will first evaluate the literature concerning the relationship between compliance and security, and then we will analyze the data gained from the review of selected studies and interviews with relevant stakeholders. Given that the majority of previous works on the topic have mainly focused on how and whether companies comply with regulations, we will develop a different strategy by basing our research on the root causes of the debate over compliance and security. In order to compare and categorize the observed results, we will use qualitative methodologies aimed at highlighting practical issues and providing recommendations. In the following sections, we present in detail the methods that will be used during each of the stages, in accordance with the research objectives and hypotheses.

Stage 1: Literature Review
Learning from experiences with safety and safety regulations, as well as early experiences with interactions between compliance and cybersecurity.

We want to build on previous research that has relevance to this project. Generally, regulations and laws are created when it is necessary to regulate, control, or stop situations or issues affecting individuals. For example, the introduction of rules to encourage improvements in the health and worker safety area has strongly redefined and influenced the concept of safety over the years, from reducing stress and risks of incidents/occupational injuries in the workplace to the development of more comprehensive insurance plans. Regulations on safety represented a departure from which regulators defined rules on cybersecurity and cyber risk. When it came to dealing with the first major cybersecurity issues, there has been a strong legislative and regulatory reaction in some countries, which led to results thanks to the existing studies on safety. Thus, although the efforts to improve the safety and security of individuals through laws and regulations have taken different approaches, they seem to have similar principles and origins. For this reason, this study will first review the literature related to the various aspects of the compliance versus safety debate in different sectors, such as health, worker safety, and construction industries. Subsequently, the literature related to the compliance versus security issue will be examined. An initial report on this part of the research plan has been completed [18].

Stage 2: Learning from Actual Experiences of Interactions Between Compliance and Security
Existing compliance/security-related management practices will be identified based on a comprehensive understanding of the most common industry practices and academic researches. This will be performed by reviewing case study papers and statistical reports. Additionally, existing regulations will be analyzed along with potential costs and risks involved in implementing the requirements associated with specific regulations. This will involve identifying the related controls and whether or not there are relevant differences between the presence or absence of these controls in terms of cyber risks. The results will be compared with recent attacks.

Stage 3: Collect and Analyze Data from Companies
The third stage of this research involves collecting and analyzing data from companies to investigate the role compliance in function of cybersecurity within their organizational systems. The primary research method for gathering data for this study will be research surveys, where data for different organizations are collected through methods, such as questionnaires, interviews, and published information. Companies will have the opportunity to use the questions of the survey as a self-assessment method and compare their results with the framework developed in the final stage of this research. In particular, data will be acquired from organizations belonging to two major categories: large enterprises and small-to-medium-sized organizations. The survey will be useful to understand whether compliance has a positive or negative influence on the organizations' cybersecurity posture and hence to provide generalizable results about the object of this study. The diverse outcomes will be analyzed in the context of different industries, locations, situations and organizational structures. Therefore, we will use case studies as a method of inquiry to inform our plan's development, highlighting the role played by compliance and, thus, the close connection between regulations and security.

Stage 4: Framework
In this stage, a framework will be created to organize and present the data and insights gained. In fact, early versions of possible frameworks will be used to help focus and organize the data gathering process. This framework will be used to analyze and compare the cases (circa 10). We will then implement a qualitative comparative analysis to identify the conditions under which compliance represents a positive o negative factor in relation to cybersecurity.

Stage 5: Recommendations
The culmination of this research will be a set of recommendations for organizations. This will help managers and executives make more informed decisions and get a sense of whether their organization has an accurate understanding of their compliance impact on their cybersecurity environment. Comparison between these categories may be performed through the analysis of a number of organizational level factors that have an impact on the interplay between compliance and cybersecurity. Criteria may include organizational structure, business model, geopolitical diversity, reporting structure, market/industry type, etc.

5   Intended Impact

Most executives assume that just because their organizations are compliant, they are automatically secure. While this may be true in some cases, managing security with a "checkbox mentality" may often result in inadequate protection. This paper has the purpose to address this issue and provide executives with the right tools to change this assumption. This research intends to achieve this by investigating the best way to develop the maximum benefit of synergy between cybersecurity and compliance. Particularly, the study has the following sub-objectives:

1. To provide a comprehensive overview of the main challenges facing organizations in balancing compliance and security;
2. To review current industry researches and practices regarding the role of compliance in security management;
3. To outline a conceptual framework for management to attain best compliance and security.

The result of this study will be valuable to executives as well as consulting organizations in developing better practices and tools for helping organizations avoid unrealistic expectations about their resilience capabilities and reduce the challenges connected to compliance and cybersecurity. Additionally, this research could be the foundation to build a network of organizations that could be interested in sharing their issues on compliance/security and finding solutions. This aspect could also be an incentive for companies to participate in this study.

Acknowledgements. The research reported herein was supported in part by the Cybersecurity at MIT Sloan initiative, which is funded by a consortium of organizations, and a gift from C6 bank.

References

1. Antonialli, D., Souza Abreu, J.: InternetLab Files Amicus Brief to Microsoft Warrant Case in the US Supreme Court. InternetLab. http://www.internetlab.org.br/en/privacy-and-sur veillance/internetlab-files-amicus-brief-to-microsoft-warrant-case-in-the-us-supreme-court (2018). Accessed 20 Nov 2020
2. Alfawaz, S., Nelson, K., Mohannak, K.: Information security culture: a behaviour compliance conceptual framework. In: Information Security 2010: AISC 2010 Proceedings of the Eighth Australasian Conference on Information Security [Conferences in Research and Practice in Information Technology, Volume 105], pp. 51–60. Australian Computer Society (2010)
3. Aurigemma, S., Panko, R.: A composite framework for behavioral compliance with information security policies. In: 2012 45th Hawaii International Conference on System Sciences, pp. 3248–3257. IEEE (2012)
4. Bartol, N., O'Malley, B., Bickford, J., Coden, M.: Radically Simplifying Regulatory Compliance in Cybersecurity. Boston Consulting Group (2019). https://www.bcg.com/en-ch/cap abilities/technology-digital/simplifying-compliance-in-cybersecurity.aspx. Accessed 11 Oct 2020
5. Abramatic, J.F.: Privacy bridges. In: 37th International Privacy Conference Amsterdam (2015). https://privacybridges.mit.edu/sites/default/files/documents/PrivacyBridges-FINAL. pdf
6. Bulgurcu, B., Cavusoglu, H., Benbasat, I.: Information security policy compliance: an empirical study of rationality-based beliefs and information security awareness. MIS Q. **34**(3), 523–548 (2010)
7. A Charter of Fundamental Rights of the European Union: Official Journal of the European Communities (2000). http://www.europarl.europa.eu/charter/pdf/text_en.pdf. Accessed 10 Nov 2020
8. Financial Services Sector Cybersecurity Profile v.10: an Overview and User Guide: Financial Services Sector Coordinating Council for Critical Infrastructure Protection and Homeland Security (2018). https://www.fsscc.org/files/galleries/Financial_Services_Sector_Cybersecu rity_Profile_Overview_and_User_Guide_2018-10-25.pdf. Accessed 10 Nov 2020

9. GDPR and Brexit- are You Sure you are Compliant? (2018). Simplisys. https://www.simpli sys.co.uk/news/gdpr-brexit-sure-compliant/. Accessed 10 Nov 2020

10. Gross, G.: Update: Breach Exposes Data on 110 Million Customers, Target Now Says, Computer World (2014). https://www.computerworld.com/article/2487587/update--breach-exposes-data-on-110-million-customers--target-now-says.html. Accessed 10 Nov 2020

11. Gürses, S.: Can you engineer privacy? Commun. ACM **57**(8), 20–23 (2014). https://limo. libis.be/primo-explore/fulldisplay?docid=LIRIAS1662104&context=L&vid=Lirias&sea rch_scope=Lirias&tab=default_tab&lang=en_US&fromSitemap=1

12. Hwang, I., Kim, D., Kim, T., Kim, S.: Why not comply with information security? An empirical approach for the causes of non-compliance. Online Information Review (2017)

13. Johnson, L.: Infosecurity Europe 2017 Survey Report-GDPR. AT&T (2017). https://www. alienvault.com/who-we-are/press-releases/infosecurity-europe-2017-survey-report-gdpr. Accessed 10 Nov 2020

14. Julisch, K.: Security compliance: the next frontier in security research. In: Proceedings of the 2008 New Security Paradigms Workshop, pp. 71–74 (2008)

15. Krebs, B.: Transcription Service Leaked Medical Records. Krebson Security (2018). https:// krebsonsecurity.com/2018/04/transcription-service-leaked-medical-records/. Accessed 10 Nov 2020

16. Kwon, J., Johnson, M.E.: The impact of security practices on regulatory Compliance and security performance. In: Proceedings of the 32nd International Conference on Information Systems, AIS (2011)

17. Marotta, A., Pearlson, K.: A culture of cybersecurity at Banca Popolare di Sondrio. In: Proceedings of AMCIS 2019 (Americas Conference on Information Systems) (2019). https:// aisel.aisnet.org/amcis2019/info_security_privacy/info_security_privacy/24/

18. Marotta, A., Madnick, S.: Analyzing the interplay between regulatory compliance and cyber-security. In: 19th Annual Security Conference, Las Vegas, NV (2020). http://dx.doi.org/10. 2139/ssrn.3542563

19. Moldes, C.J.: PCI DSS and Security Breaches: Preparing for a Security Breach that Affects Cardholder Data. SANS Institute (2018). https://www.sans.org/readingroom/whitepapers/bre aches/pci-dss-security-breaches-preparing-security-breachaffects-cardholder-data-38340

20. Moody, G.D., Siponen, M., Pahnila, S.: Toward a unified model of information security policy compliance. MIS Q. **42**(1) (2018)

21. Morrow, L.: SolarWinds Federal Cybersecurity Survey Summary Report, SolarWinds, Market Connections, Slideshare.net (2017). https://www.slideshare.net/SolarWinds/solarw inds-federal-cybersecurity-survey-2017-government-regulations-it-modernization-and-car eless-insiders-undermine-federal-agencies-security-posture/1. Accessed 10 Nov 2020

22. New Cybersecurity Industry Survey Exposes Widespread Concern about Upcoming GDPR (2018). GDPR. https://eugdpr.com/news/new-cybersecurity-industry-survey-exposes-widesp read-concern-upcoming-gdpr/. Accessed 10 Nov 2020

23. PCI and DSS Requirement 1- Install & Maintain a Firewall Configuration (2020). PCI-Guide. https://www.pci-guide.co.uk/section-1.html. Accessed 10 Nov 2020

24. Report on Cybersecurity Practices. (2015). Financial Industry Regulatory Author-ity. https://www.finra.org/sites/default/files/p602363%20Report%20on%20Cybersecurity% 20Practices_0.pdf. Accessed 10 Nov 2020

25. Safa, N.S., Von Solms, R., Furnell, S.: Information security policy compliance model in organizations. Comput. Secur. **56**, 70–82 (2016)

26. Scorsim, E.M.: Brazil and the United States of America: Jurisdiction and the Application of Domestic Laws on Internet Application and Technology Companies. Mgalhas Interna-tional. https://www.migalhas.com/HotTopics/63,MI273592,61044-Brazil+and+the+United+ States+of+America+Jurisdiction+and+the (2018). Accessed 10 Nov 2020

27. Sommestad, T., Hallberg, J., Lundholm, K., Bengtsson, J.: Variables influencing information security policy compliance. Inf. Manage. Comput. Secur. (2014)
28. Stefanelli, S.: First GDPR Sanctions are Underway: The German Case. Europrivacy. Blog.europrivacy.info (2018). https://europrivacy.info/2018/12/15/first-gdpr-sanctions-are-underway-the-german-case/. Accessed 10 Nov 2020
29. Vance, A., Siponen, M., Pahnila, S.: Motivating IS security compliance: insights from habit and protection motivation theory. Inf. Manage. (2012). http://130.18.86.27/faculty/warkentin/SecurityPapers/Newer/VanceSiponenPahnila012_I&M49_HabitPMT.pdf
30. Vroom, C., Von Solms, R.: Towards information security behavioural compliance. Comput. Secur. **23**(3), 191–198 (2004)
31. Woodside, S.: How not to do Healthcare Security. Medstack (2018). https://medstack.co/blog/not-healthcare-security/. Accessed 10 Nov 2020

Developing a Framework for Hotel IT Investment Decision-Making Amid COVID-19

Yu-Hsiang (John) Huang[1]([✉]), Daniel Connolly[1], Tianshu Zheng[2], and Yu-Ju Tu[3]

[1] Drake University, Des Moines, USA
yu-hsiang.huang@drake.edu
[2] Iowa State University, Ames, USA
[3] National Chengchi University, Taipei, Taiwan

Abstract. Travel fears and restrictions, imposed capacity limitations, and the inability to hold events and large group gatherings have stifled hotel demand and caused devastating revenue losses for the hotel industry during the COVID-19 pandemic. The financial losses will undoubtedly affect hotel firms' information technology (IT) investments in the long run. This paper aims to develop a framework to assist hotel executives in capturing more insights regarding the relationship between input resources and desired outputs throughout the production process. Accordingly, hotel executives will be able to evaluate and make appropriate IT investment decisions to strategically and effectively allocate scare financial resources in order to improve firm performance.

Keywords: Hotel IT investments · Decision-making · Coronavirus (COVID-19) · Firm performance

1 Introduction

The U.S. unemployment rate reached a staggering 25% amid the coronavirus (COVID-19) pandemic, and the reported numbers may get worse before getting better (Macias 2020). The *USA Today* reported that the pandemic has resulted in nearly 80% of the U.S. hotel room inventory going vacant. For many hotels, including those in the top 25 U.S. markets, occupancy rates have dipped into single digits (Oliver 2020), contributing to the temporary and permanent closures of many hotels, including some iconic ones (e.g., Los Angeles' Luxe Rodeo Drive Hotel, Chicago's Palmer House Hilton, and New York's Hilton Times Square). After rebounding from the 2008 recession and recovering from 9/11, the U.S. hotel industry once again is facing a severe global economic crisis caused by COVID-19. Compared to the same week in 2019, the U.S. revenue per available room (RevPar) in the week of May 2nd dropped by 76.8% to $21.39 (STR. U.S. Hotel Results, May 2020), forcing the hotel industry to reduce expenses and minimize capital expenditures in the near term. Loannou and Flammer (2019) found that most U.S. publicly traded firms significantly reduced expenses and capital expenditures (CAPEX) during

© Springer Nature Switzerland AG 2021
A. Garimella et al. (Eds.): WeB 2020, LNBIP 418, pp. 25–31, 2021.
https://doi.org/10.1007/978-3-030-79454-5_3

the 2008 Great Recession. However, they also suggested that while reducing CAPEX, companies continued to invest in R&D (research and development) to respond to the crisis by "investing their way out of the crisis." This suggests that companies would continue investing in innovative and sustainable projects to meet future market and customer demand despite lower earnings and tighter budget during economic downturns.

Technology decision-making is considered to be a multifarious process before the approval and funding support are granted in the hospitality industry (Cobanoglu et al. 2013). Among many investment decisions hotel executives must make, information technology (IT) investments are highly complex because they are so intertwined and integral to nearly every business process. Moreover, they are often context-specific, with outcomes dependent upon the type of IT investment, the characteristics surrounding the project, and user adoption, among other factors. Thus, the IT investment decision requires hotel executives to be well versed in technology in order to evaluate various technology-related initiatives with keen business acumen and an eye toward risk (e.g., Connolly 1999; Marriott 2016). Further, the use of self-service technologies is likely to be inevitable for the foreseeable future given the rise in mobile technologies, proposed increases in the minimum wage, and the desire for contactless service during the pandemic. Additionally, investing in artificial intelligence projects will be critical for the hotel industry to meet upcoming customer expectations and find new ways to create operating efficiencies and reduce labor costs. These and other technological advances are driving change throughout all facets of the hotel industry—from how business is transacted to how services are delivered—while at the same time, putting increased pressure on hotel executives to invest in more technology to keep pace with customer demands, competitor moves, and employee expectations (e.g., Nyheim and Connolly 2011; Cobanoglu et al. 2013). Therefore, this study seeks to answer the following research question: How can hotel executives make better IT investment decisions, ones that will contribute to ongoing growth during the COVID-19 pandemic and lead to improved firm performance? To address this issue, our study reviews hotel IT investment-related studies to develop a theoretical framework that incorporates the relevant input and output variables (see Sect. 2). Future directions for this study are discussed in Sect. 3.

2   Literature Review

Determining and measuring the expected and actual contributions provided by IT may vary in different disciplines (e.g., Kauffman et al. 2015; Steelman et al. 2019). IT investment decisions often require more involvement than other investment decisions in terms of the number of people and areas of the organization due to their impact. In this section, we present a literature review of hotel IT investment-related studies. Based on specific characteristics identified in the literature, this study develops a framework built upon a production process that incorporates three categories: (1) IT budget, (2) general hotel performance indicators, and (3) risk as shown below.

2.1 IT Budget

Due to limited resources in the era of COVID-19, hotel executives are expected to allocate their firms' resources more efficiently while keeping the business running smoothly. Since the budget is highly correlated to a firm's invested resources, numerous studies (e.g., Grover et al. 1998; Kohli and Grover 2008) show that achieving IT payoffs requires thoughtful integration of business strategy, people, processes, guest expectations, and IT to achieve the organization's desired results. The benefits of new technology developments can often take several years to realize (e.g., Law et al. 2009; Cobanoglu et al. 2013). It is clearly noted that the budget for IT investments is a concern shared by both IT and business executives. For example, some of the latest industry reports suggest that chief financial officers (CFOs) have sought to update the upper limits (i.e., the cap limits) for their IT investment budgets because economic prospects had significantly changed. They also recognize their firms' increased reliance on technology in order to maintain business continuity and serve guests in a safe manner (Van Der Meulen 2020).

Relatedly, many scholars have proposed that an IT budget can be one effective instrument for governing the overall IT functions in organization (e.g., Keil 1995; Lacity and Willcocks 1998; Lee et al. 2004) and lead to better alignment between the IT function and the core disciplines of the firm (i.e., accounting, finance, sales, marketing, operations, management, etc.), especially if the firm has a cross-functional IT steering committee in place. At the hotel firm level, IT expenses can be regarded as the technology-related costs (e.g., personnel, computer hardware, software, and network costs) that a hotel company incurs when performing its normal business operations and the day-to-day expense of running the hotel company's IT function. Through the IT budget, IT expenses could be grouped by type of system (e.g., property management system, point-of-sale, and mobile) or area (e.g., guest experience, security, infrastructure, back-of-house, and administrative).

An established best practice according to MIS (management information systems) literature (e.g., Chan et al. 1997; Aral and Weill 2007; Xue et al. 2012), is to apply a portfolio approach to allocate and manage IT spending and IT investments. This approach will also help executives to better manage risks associated with IT projects, allocate staff across projects, and minimize disruption that new IT projects can have on business operations. Strategic alignment is critical to the selection of IT projects added to the portfolio (Cho and Shaw 2013; Karhade et al. 2015). Therefore, hotel firms that consider IT investments using a portfolio approach can better match their IT investments to strategic objectives and risk profiles (e.g., Maizlish and Handler 2005; Weill and Aral 2006), resulting in stronger outcomes, greater satisfaction, and enhanced firm performance.

2.2 General Hotel Performance Indicators

General hotel performance indicators include revenue per available room (RevPar), occupancy percentage, and guest satisfaction index. Firstly, revenue per available room (RevPar) is simply room revenue divided by the number of rooms available (Chikish et al. 2017); it is an important measurement of the balance between hotel room supply and demand or yield (Hua and Yang 2017). Secondly, occupancy percentage is the number of rooms sold divided by the total number of rooms available. It is a measurement of both demand for rooms and supply for rooms (Chikish et al. 2017). Since occupancy percentages at hotels are constrained, managers must make decisions regarding pricing and demand to maximize overall revenue (Anderson and Lawrence 2014). In other words, occupancy percentage is the percentage of rooms that are occupied on a given night. Thirdly, Gundersen et al. (1996) defined consumer (guest) satisfaction as a post consumption evaluative judgment concerning a specific product or service. The guest satisfaction index can vary by hotel company but is essentially a composite score based upon guest feedback captured from a survey administered post stay. It is intended to provide continuous improvement data to hotels while serving as an indicator of guests' intent to return (i.e., loyalty). Lastly, while implementing IT investment projects in hotel companies, cost savings can be used to estimate the expected return from business process improvement and inventory reduction.

2.3 Risk

Risk is a multi-dimensional term. In general, risks (e.g., financial, operational, and business) are modeled on the basis of the impact of an unwanted outcome under uncertain conditions, and risk is perceived as the possibility of additional cost or loss due to the choice of alternatives (e.g., Pearlson and Saunders 2010; Wang et al. 2010). Furthermore, risk is a critical piece when assessing IT investment projects (e.g., Huang et al. 2019; Tu et al. 2020). Understanding investments in IT projects is of great importance for hotel executives, who generally believe there is a high degree of risk with IT projects due to the lack of industrywide benchmarks and technical complexity (Connolly 1999). Risk associated with IT projects include financial risk (that a project will come in over budget), functional risk (that the project will fail to deliver the expected functionality), and opportunity costs (that the project will be completed late, resulting in missed business opportunities or competitive disadvantage).

Much of the study of productivity is based on input-output models. Prior research shows that production theory has been widely utilized in assessing the productivity to uncover how best to combine resource inputs to achieve desired results (outputs). Specifically, Ayabakan et al. (2017) explore the impact of IT on operational capabilities in the context of production processes. To apply the production process to IT investment decisions in the hospitality industry, our study extends David et al.'s (1996) work to develop a research framework that incorporates three categories (i.e., IT budget, general hotel performance indicators, and risk) and classify them as either input variables or output variables throughout the production process as shown in Fig. 1.

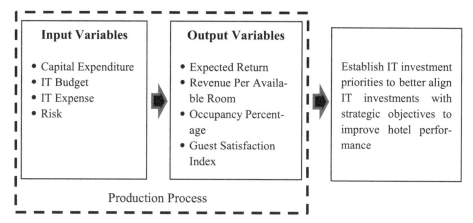

Fig. 1. Framework of IT investment variables in the hotel industry

3 Discussion and Future Direction

In the era of COVID-19, changing times and increased technology dependence require more infrastructure, security, and support. COVID-19 will forever change the hotel industry. The immediate future of the hotel industry is ominous with recovery expected to take years, not months. Regrettably, some hotels, as we have already seen, will never be able to recover, and more hotel closures are likely to occur in the coming months given the prolonged nature of the pandemic and its lingering aftereffects. That said, the hotel industry is known to be resilient, as history has revealed (e.g., the recoveries from 2008 recession and after 9/11). To emerge from this pandemic, hotels will introduce new operating practices and rely more heavily on technology to serve guest needs while keeping them and their employees safe. In practice, the hotel industry has been focused on contactless service delivered via technology. An interesting conundrum for hotels is that they need to invest more in technology to deliver services in a safe manner during the pandemic; however, they lack the budgets to support these investments in technology—especially with occupancy rates being so low. Hence, the contribution of our study is to develop a framework that will enable hotel executives to capture more insights regarding the relationship between input resources and desired outputs in the IT investment decision process in order to enhance their decision-making effectiveness. In line with the proposed framework, our future direction intends to build a quantitative model to assist hotel executives in establishing IT investment priorities and allocating scare resources to improve firm performance.

References

Anderson, C.K., Lawrence, B.: The influence of online reputation and product heterogeneity on service firm financial performance. Serv. Sci. **6**(4), 217–228 (2014)

Aral, S., Weill, P.: IT assets, organizational capabilities, and firm performance: how resource allocations and organizational differences explain performance variation. Organ. Sci. **18**(1), 763–780 (2007)

Ayabakan, S., Bardhan, I.R., Zheng, Z.E.: A data envelopment analysis approach to estimate IT-enabled production capability. MIS Q. **41**(1), 189–205 (2017)

Chan, Y., Huff, S., Barclay, D., Copeland, D.: Business strategic orientation, information systems strategic orientation, and strategic alignment. Inf. Syst. Res. **8**(2), 125–150 (1997)

Chikish, Y., Humphreys, B., Liu, C., Nowak, A.: Professional sports events, concerts, and urban place based policy: evidence from the staples center. Working paper No. 17–32, Department of Economics, West Virginia University (2017)

Cho, W., Shaw, M.: Portfolio selection model for enhancing information technology synergy. IEEE Trans. Eng. Manag. **60**(4), 739–749 (2013)

Cobanoglu, C., Ayoun, B., Connolly, D., Nusair, K.: The effect of information technology steering committees on perceived IT management sophistication in hotels. Int. J. Hosp. Tour. Adm. **14**(1), 1–22 (2013)

Connolly, D.: Understanding information technology investment decision-making in the context of hotel global distribution systems: a multiple-case study. Dissertation, Virginia Polytechnic Institute and State University (1999)

David, J.S., Grabski, S., Kasavana, M.: The productivity paradox of hotel-industry technology. Cornell Hotel Restaurant Admin. Q. **37**(2), 64–70 (1996)

Grover, V., Teng, J.T., Fiedler, K.D.: IS investment priorities in contemporary organizations. Commun. ACM **41**(2), 40–48 (1998)

Gundersen, M.G., Heide, M., Olsson, U.H.: Hotel guest satisfaction among business travelers: what are the important factors? Cornell Hotel and Restaurant Admin. Q. **37**(2), 72–81 (1996)

Hua, N., Yang, Y.: Systematic effects of crime on hotel operating performance. Tour. Manag. **60**, 257–269 (2017)

Huang, Y.H., Tu, Y.J., Strader, T.J., Shaw, M.J., Subramanyam, R.R.: Selecting the most desirable IT portfolio under various risk tolerance levels. Inf. Resour. Manag. J. **32**(4), 1–19 (2019)

Karhade, P., Shaw, M.J., Subramanyam, R.: Patterns in information systems portfolio prioritization: evidence from decision tree induction. MIS Q. **39**(2), 413–434 (2015)

Kauffman, R.J., Liu, J., Ma, D.: Technology investment decision-making under uncertainty. Inf. Technol. Manage. **16**(2), 153–172 (2015). https://doi.org/10.1007/s10799-014-0212-2

Keil, M.: Pulling the plug: software project management and the problem of project escalation. MIS Q. **19**(4), 421–447 (1995)

Kohli, R., Grover, V.: Business value of IT: an essay on expanding research directions to keep up with the times. J. Assoc. Inf. Syst. **9**(1), 23–39 (2008)

Lacity, M.C., Willcocks, L.P.: An empirical investigation of information technology sourcing practices: lessons from experience. MIS Q. **22**(1), 363–408 (1998)

Law, R., Leung, R., Buhalis, D.: Information technology applications in hospitality and tourism: a review of publications from 2005 to 2007. J. Travel Tour. Mark. **26**(5–6), 599–623 (2009)

Lee, J., Miranda, S., Kim, Y.: IT outsourcing strategies: universalistic, contingency, and configurational explanations of success. Inf. Syst. Res. **15**(2), 110–131 (2004)

Loannou, I., Flammer, C.: Save or invest? how companies should navigate recessions. https://hbr.org/2019/05/save-or-invest-how-companies-should-navigate-recessions. Accessed 1 Aug 2020

Macias, A.: Mnuchin says jobless numbers will 'get worse before they get better'—unemployment may have hit 25%. https://www.cnbc.com/2020/05/10/coronavirus-mnuchin-says-unemployment-will-rate-get-worse-before-they-get-better.html. Accessed 15 Sep 2020

Maizlish, B., Handler, R.: IT Portfolio Management Step-By-Step: Unlocking the Business Value of Technology. John Wiley & Sons, Hoboken (2005)

Marriott, S.: Considerations for a hotel investment. Thesis, University of Nevada, Las Vegas (2016)

Nyheim, P., Connolly, D.: Technology Strategies for The Hospitality Industry. Prentice Hall Press, Upper Saddle River (2011)

Oliver, D.: About 80% of hotel rooms in the US are empty amid the coronavirus pandemic, new data says. https://www.usatoday.com/story/travel/hotels/2020/04/09/coronavirus-leaves-hotel-rooms-empty-str-data/5120441002/. Accessed 15 Sep 2020

Pearlson, K., Saunders, C.S.: Managing and Using Information Systems: A Strategic Approach. John Wiley & Sons, Hoboken (2010)

Steelman, Z.R., Havakhor, T., Sabherwal, R., Sabherwal, S.: Performance consequences of information technology investments: implications of emphasizing new or current information technologies. Inf. Syst. Res. **30**(1), 204–218 (2019)

STR. U.S. hotel results for week ending 2 May. https://str.com/press-release/str-us-hotel-results-week-ending-2-may. Accessed 1 Sep 2020

Tu, Y.J., Huang, Y.H., Strader, T.J., Subramanyam, R., Shaw, M.J.: Candidate diversity and granularity in IT portfolio construction. Inf. Technol. Manage. **21**(3), 157–168 (2020). https://doi.org/10.1007/s10799-019-00312-1

Van Der Meulen, R.: Gartner CFO survey reveals that 62% of CFOs plan SG&A cuts this year due to coronavirus related disruptions. https://www.gartner.com/en/newsroom/press-releases/2020-04-06-gartner-cfo-survey-reveals-that-62-percent-of-cfos-plan-sganda-cuts-this-year-due-to-coronavirus. Accessed 15 Sep 2020

Wang, J., Lin, W., Huang, Y.H.: A performance oriented risk management framework for innovative R&D projects. Technovation **30**(11), 601–611 (2010)

Weill, P., Aral, S.: Generating premium returns on your IT investments. MIT Sloan Manag. Rev. **47**(2), 39–48 (2006)

Xue, L., Ray, G., Sambamurthy, V.: Efficiency or innovation: how do industry environments moderate the effects of firms' IT asset portfolios? MIS Q. **36**(2), 509–528 (2012)

Examining the Effect of Experience on Managers' Attitudes Towards Telework During COVID

Henri Knoesen[✉] and Lisa F. Seymour

Department of IS, University of Cape Town, Cape Town, South Africa
henri.knoesen@alumni.uct.ac.za, Lisa.seymour@uct.ac.za

Abstract. Improvements in technology over the past two decades have increased the ability of employees to work remotely however there has been a hesitation on the part of organizations and managers to allow this practice. In response to the Covid-19 lockdown, companies were forced to adopt teleworking arrangements for their entire workforce. Research has demonstrated that managers are the gatekeepers of adoption and diffusion decisions in organizations. This study investigates whether managers that experienced telework in their teams over the mandated lockdown period changed their perceptions of telework and willingness to allow their staff to work remotely and describes their perceptions. A survey was sent to managers twice within a four-month period in a single case organization in South Africa that was forced to allow the entire workforce to telework. The results of the study found that when managers had experienced telework for four months, they were more in favour of supporting this working arrangement in the organization. Yet teleworking is not without its challenges which this study highlights.

Keywords: Telework · Telecommuting · e-work · Work from home

1 Introduction

The Covid-19 pandemic of 2020 changed all aspects of normal life across the globe. One of the biggest changes experienced by people and organizations was the inability to go to work as governments forced mandatory lockdowns and people were made to stay home. While telework, which is also known as telecommuting, remote work, home-based work, e-work, or nomadic work, to name but a few (Beham et al. 2014; van der Merwe and Smith 2014) has been a popular topic and practice in organisations as well as academic literature for several decades, the pandemic raised its importance to an all-time high. The expected adoption of telework by organizations before the pandemic was largely unrealised as adoption rates have been much lower than expected (van der Merwe and Smith 2014). Advances in Information and Communication Technology (ICT) solutions have created renewed interest in teleworking in recent years but more importantly it is these solutions that have helped organisations find ways of working during this unprecedented global disruption (Agerfalk et al. 2020) during which teleworking changed from an option to

© Springer Nature Switzerland AG 2021
A. Garimella et al. (Eds.): WeB 2020, LNBIP 418, pp. 32–47, 2021.
https://doi.org/10.1007/978-3-030-79454-5_4

that of necessity. The adoption of telework has been previously underscored as a critical component of business continuity after disruption to normal business operations (Green et al. 2017; Martin and McDonnell 2012).

There is an abundance of literature which discusses the need for management support when organisations adopt telework practices. Studies highlight the need for a positive attitude towards teleworking from managers since it requires that they have a different set of skills when managing remote workers and direct supervisors usually influence whether employees can work from home or not (Beham et al. 2014; Silva et al. 2019). While this voluntary willingness of managers to support telework was the case prior to the Covid-19 pandemic, the lockdown forced organisations and managers to adopt telework for the entire workforce in most companies within days. Covid-19 created an unprecedented opportunity to examine the phenomenon of telework and its adoption and impact on organisations on a scale which never existed previously. Studies have demonstrated that as manager's awareness of telework and its benefits increases, greater levels of telework adoption can be expected in organizations (van der Merwe and Smith 2014). Therefore, if telework is to be implemented and accepted throughout an organization, it is imperative that managers have a positive attitude towards it. This paper explores the experience of one case organization that rapidly adopted teleworking for its entire workforce following the mandatory Covid-19 lockdown. The purpose was to explore whether the attitudes of managers towards teleworking changed between the start of the lockdown and when employees were first allowed to return to the office several months later.

The paper will be structured as follows. The next section discusses the state of knowledge regarding why telework is adopted, and how its adoption is impeded or facilitated by the attitudes of managers within organizations. This will be followed by the method used for the study and thereafter the discussion of the findings.

2   Literature Review

Telework has been defined in four dimensions; the locations from where the work is done, the use of technology, the amount of time spent between the remote location and the office, and the type of contractual relationship between the employee and employer (Silva et al. 2019). The traditional understanding of telework is where work is done from any location other than the organization's premises. This includes the home of the employee; mobile locations such as coffee shops, airports, hotels; or specialized locations which are designed for nomadic workers (Silva et al. 2019). The conditions under which this study was conducted was during the government mandated country-wide lockdown in South Africa where all employees were forced to work from home. At the time of writing this paper, most employees were still working from home.

Telework Benefits

Telework literature categorizes benefits accruing to individuals, organizations and society (Green et al. 2017). Individual benefits cited include greater autonomy which leads to improved work-life balance, more favourable work environments, and reduced expenses (Nakrosiene et al. 2019). Organizational benefits reported include greater agility derived from virtual teams, reduced employee turnover, improved customer service, higher productivity and efficiency through lower absenteeism, and improved organizational performance (Greer and Payne 2014; Morikawa 2018; Silva et al. 2019). The societal benefits are created from the environmental impact of reduced traffic volumes and land usage (van der Merwe and Smith 2014). Yet studies show that despite the awareness of the possible benefits and the existence of formal policies allowing remote work in organizations, the allowance of these arrangements is often at the discretion of managers (Beham et al. 2014). Prior to the pandemic, these arrangements were mostly voluntary with the aim of giving workers flexibility in managing their time. Companies also offered telework as an incentive to attract scare skills in an ever increasingly competitive job market (Beham et al. 2014).

Conditions and Capabilities for Telework Support

For managers to embrace telework as an option for their employees, several conditions have been identified by Silva et al. (2019): the perceived usefulness of teleworking explained by the benefits for both the employees and the organization; the ease with which telework can be implemented in the organization; the social pressures of the community in which the manager operates such as family commitments, legislation, mobility factors in cities, and environmental impact considerations; the importance of work and the compatibility of telework to the job being done; facilitating conditions in the organisation to support teleworking such as technological and administrative support to enable measurement, supervision and control of remote workers; and self-efficacy of the employees to support themselves such as in resolving technical issues and managing their time.

Managers as Gatekeepers

The term 'discretionary decisions of managers' was coined by Beham et al. (2014) in relation to the telework allowance decisions which managers make as the gatekeepers allowing staff to telework. Management concerns over opportunistic behaviour by employees is often cited as a disincentive for telework support (van der Merwe and Smith 2014). Tework changes the power balance between employees and managers since employees get to decide where and when to work and managers lose that control over their staff (Beham et al. 2014). Managers can experience this loss of control as anxiety since they can no longer evaluate employee performance through direct observation (Thompson 2008). Additionally, the change in how they communicate, monitor, and coordinate effort with remote workers potentially causes trepidation towards telework (Collins et al. 2016). Management control and trust have been shown to be correlated with telework adoption (Lebopo et al. 2020). The belief that telework makes managing employees more difficult makes it less likely that managers will encourage and allow it for their employees (Beham et al. 2014). Prior experience with telework was found to have a significant and positive influence on the attitude of managers towards the practice (Silva et al. 2019). If managers experienced telework and managed remote workers in the past, they were found to have a more favourable attitude towards it. Therefore, this study aimed to test the hypothesis:

H1: As managers' telework experience increases their attitude towards the practice becomes more favourable.

Organisational Culture and Practice

Even though telework is enabled by ICT, it is first and foremost a workplace and organizational innovation that requires significant investment and effort in changing practices and policies for managing employees (van der Merwe and Smith 2014). Telework needs to fit with the organisation's IT infrastructure and its management norms and values (Lebopo et al. 2020). While ordinarily it is managers who determine whether telework can be adopted into a role (Bentley et al. 2013) and managers that influence telework habits within organizations, business interruption following natural disasters or other unexpected events in an organization's environment, necessitates the adoption of telework to enhance the organization's adaptive capability (Green et al. 2017; Martin and McDonnell 2012). This does not imply that the role of managers in supporting telework is diminished in these situations, the implementation is still reliant on their attitude toward telework (Beham et al. 2014; Nakosiene et al. 2019). There have been calls for studies which examine organizational factors that affect adoption and subsequent diffusion of telework within the organization as telework matures (van der Merwe and Smith 2014) and also for empirical studies which examine the outcomes of implementing telework following disaster situations with respect to organizations, groups, and individuals (Green et al. 2017). This study addresses these two needs by describing telework experiences and examining whether the managers in the case organization changed their attitudes towards telework during the pandemic.

3   Method

This exploratory study utilized a survey instrument within a single organization case by means of a survey instrument which was used to collect data at two different intervals, four months apart. Through the two surveys (S1 and S2), both quantitative and qualitative data was collected. After a review of the literature, three dominant theoretical themes were identified and questions on these themes were asked. One hypothesis was proposed and tested.

The case study is of a South African insurer. The company has approximately 4000 employees distributed mainly in two major cities, Cape Town and Johannesburg, with the head office situated in Cape Town. At the end of March 2020, the South African government put the entire country into a compulsory lockdown whereby nobody could leave their homes except to purchase essential items such as food and medicine. A small number of businesses were deemed to be critical and could operate under strict conditions. With very little time to prepare for the lockdown, companies of all sizes were forced to find ICT solutions which enabled telework for those employees who had jobs that could be accomplished from home. While telework had been an established practice for some employees in this organization, most notably IT staff and more senior job grades, most of the employees especially those in lower job grades had not been allowed to work from home prior to the lockdown. Where telework had been allowed, it had been at the discretion of the line manager and the working arrangement was negotiated between the manager and the employee.

The sampling method used for the respondents was a convenience non-probability sampling design. S1 was sent to all managers (436 managerial job grades) one week after the start of the lockdown in the first week of April 2020 and S2 was sent to the same group of managers 4 months later, during August 2020. Table 1 shows the demographics of respondents. Both surveys had the same typical respondent, which was female, middle manager (Peromnes job grade 5–7), and aged 45 to 54. A job grade of 1 is an executive and 8 is a team lead or junior manager in the organization. For S1, 201 managers responded (46%), and 260 valid responses were received from S2 (60%). The lower response rate to S1 is attributed to the stress of managers at the start of the lock-down.

Table 1. Respondents by survey number

No	Age				Gender		Job grade			Total
	25–34	35–44	45–54	55–64	F	M	0–4	5–7	8+	
1	25	68	79	29	109	92	12	120	69	201
2	31	91	102	36	149	111	16	165	79	260

The quantitative data was analysed using Statistica. The non-parametric Mann-Whitney difference of means test was used to verify the differences between the responses from S1 and S2. Spearman rank correlation was used across both samples to test if Manager's attitudes varied with their age. Themes to explain the quantitative results were identified from the coding of the qualitative data using qualitative thematic analysis and HyperResearch.

4   Results and Discussion

Table 2 lists the questions asked in each survey according to each theoretical theme as well as the percentage agreement with the relevant questions. In S1 10 questions were used to collect quantitative answers and one question was used to a collect qualitative response. The second survey used the same questions as survey 1 with the addition of four quantitative questions which interrogated the post-lockdown perceptions towards telework. Q1 used a 3-point scale from 'not at all' to 'well-established', all other quantitative questions used a 5-point Likert-scale from 1 (strongly disagree) to 5 (strongly agree).Kindly note that Figures, Tables, Equations and their citations have been renumbered to maintain sequential order. Check and confirm.

Table 2. Survey Questions. Italicised question responses changed significantly. S refers to Survey.

S	Question	Theme	S1% agree	S2% agree
1,2	*7 - The organization is technologically capable of supporting telework*	Capability	*60*	*73*
1,2	9 - The same resources are available to teleworkers as to office workers		60	65
2	18 - The company has provided me with suitable equipment to telework			93
1,2	*1 - Is telework an established practice in your area?*	Culture and Practices	*85*	*67*
2	12 - Has telework become an established practice in your area over the lockdown period?			95
2	19 - Has telework changed in the company between now and prior to lockdown?		Qual	
1,2	*5 - The organization has a culture which promotes telework*		*47*	*59*
1,2	6 - The organization has mature processes to allow for telework		61	67
1,2	*2 - My staff do the same amount of work at home as they would in the office*	Managers as gatekeepers	*71*	*87*
1,2	8 - The productivity of the team is not negatively impacted by telework		66	70
1,2	3 - I trust my staff to telework		96	95
1,2	4 - My staff are able to manage themselves when teleworking		93	97
1,2	*10 - I would prefer that my staff work in the office rather than telework*		*55*	*40*
2	16 - My preference that my staff work in the office rather than telework has changed over the lockdown period			47
2	17 - Telework should be an option for employees in the company			95
1	11 - Please add any comments you believe are relevant regarding telework in the company		Qual	

Table 3. Descriptive statistics for S1 and S2

Question	Mean 1	Std. dev. 1	Mean 2	Std. dev. 2	Skewness 1	Skewness 2
Q1	2.14	0.66	1.83	0.68	−0.15	0.22
Q2	3.76	1.33	4.23	0.95	−0.94	−1.44
Q3	4.55	0.71	4.49	0.64	−2.11	−1.24
Q4	4.40	0.81	4.45	0.59	−1.89	−0.75
Q5	3.16	1.26	3.39	1.28	−0.20	−0.51
Q6	3.43	1.24	3.60	1.28	−0.54	−0.75
Q7	3.36	1.33	3.75	1.33	−0.46	−0.96
Q8	3.68	1.26	3.77	1.41	−0.70	−0.88
Q9	3.45	1.39	3.56	1.32	−0.46	−0.67
Q10	2.76	1.24	2.27	1.17	0.16	0.58

Table 4. Mann-Whitney U Test. Marked tests are significant at p < ,05000

VAR	Rank Sum S1	Rank Sum S2	U	Z	p-value	Z adjusted	Z adj p-value
Q1	52536	53955	20025	*4,30363*	*0,000017*	*4,73734*	*0,000002*
Q2	41641	64850	21340	*−3,37656*	*0,000734*	*−3,61717*	*0,000298*
Q3	48489	58002	24072	1,45052	0,146914	1,67920	0,093114
Q4	46914	59576	25646	0,34051	0,733471	0,38483	0,700363
Q5	43592	62899	23291	*−2,00112*	*0,045380*	*−2,06958*	*0,038492*
Q6	44147	62344	23846	−1,60985	0,107431	−1,68631	0,091738
Q7	41694	64796	21393	*−3,33885*	*0,000841*	*−3,49333*	*0,000477*
Q8	44414	62077	24113	−1,42162	0,155138	−1,48703	0,137008
Q9	45510	60981	25209	−0,64895	0,516374	−0,67329	0,500765
Q10	52255	54236	20306	*4,10553*	*0,000040*	*4,22783*	*0,000024*

Table 3 shows the descriptive statistics and Table 4 shows the differences between the two surveys. Responses to Q1, Q2, Q5, Q7, and Q10 between S1 and S2 showed a statistically significant difference with p-values < 0.05. The themes and their frequencies are showed in Table 5. The themes that surfaced from the qualitative responses also shifted in focus between S1 and S2. The themes in the surveys will now be discussed.

Table 5. Code frequencies

S1 code	Total	S2 code	Total
Connectivity problems	48	Need telework resources	39
Need telework resources	20	Connectivity problems	37
Prefer to telework	17	Improved productivity	36
Opportunity to mature telework	14	Prefer to telework	29
Need to trust employees	11	Happy with telework	25
Past experience with telework	11	Challenging for some	21
Happened suddenly	10	Need to trust employees	18
Improved productivity	10	New work processes needed	18
Need for management processes	9	New willingness to allow telework	15
Benefits from telework	7	Blended approach to telework	14
Happy with telework	7	Forced to allow telework	14
Business continuity	6	Opportunity to mature telework	14
Challenging for some	5	Reimburse for expenses	14
Reimburse for expenses	4	Benefits from telework	12
Improved team communication	2	Past experience with telework	12
New work processes needed	2	Need for management processes	10
Training for telework	2	Connectivity improved	9
		Improved team communication	6
		Business continuity	5
		Not all staff should telework	5
		Training for telework	3
		Need for social interaction	2

Telework Capability

The ICT infrastructure was not designed for large numbers of employees to work remotely, remote working policies and procedures were not prescribed by the organization, and processes for the management of teleworkers did not exist. To deal with the sudden demand for remote connectivity, the organization had to invest heavily in hardware and software for laptops, network infrastructure, and other ICT enablers. This was not immediately available as the lockdown started which meant that many employees could not connect to the office and this caused much frustration. As the technical problems were resolved, increasing numbers of employees were able to work from home and the organization settled into a 'new normal' way of teleworking. Without the practical capability of being able to access and manage work, telework is not possible.

In the second survey 93% of managers agreed with Q18 which asked whether the organization provided them with appropriate equipment to telework. There was no significant difference betwesssn responses to Q9 between S1 and S2 which related to whether managers believed that teleworkers had the same resources available to them as office workers. Both surveys showed that around 50% of managers believed that the resources were the same for both types of workers. While the IT infrastructure improved as lockdown progressed, some of the employees were not able to work as they did not have the appropriate equipment and facilities. The need for the provision of appropriate resources such as laptops, network connectivity, systems, furniture, and printers was the most commonly coded qualitative theme. This finding for the need for the organization to equip teleworkers with appropriate teleworking resources is confirmed in the literature (Hertel et al. 2005) and validated in this study:

'It is important that, for teleworking to work, the proper tools is made available to employees'; Many did not have laptops and we had connectivity issues'; 'Our division, if provided with the correct tools, can work completely on a remote basis'

Telework requires that organizations provide the technology and tools but also the operational processes. Collectively these enable management support and management controls which can act as moderators. This finding for the need of a telework capability is found in literature (van der Merwe and Smith 2014) is confirmed in this study. The data showed a statistical difference ($p = 0.0008$) in the responses to Q7 in the surveys relating to the belief that the organization was technologically capable of supporting telework. 73% of managers supported this statement in S2 compared to 60% before the lockdown in S1. As the lockdown started connectivity problems were the biggest concern for managers and their teams:

'Our main problem is connectivity to the systems and frustrations with poor quality conference calls'; 'Connectivity is sometimes an issue where you can't hear people properly. Microsoft Team meetings and WebEx work great, but connectivity is a huge hurdle'

A large amount of effort and resources were spent on improving the connectivity issue in the first weeks of lockdown and this contributed to the improved perception of telework capability:

"The organization is technologically capable to support telework; 'Apart from connectivity issues, which has improved tremendously, we have been able to work remotely'

Impact on Productivity

Improved productivity is a benefit of telework that is confirmed in many previous studies (Beham et al. 2014; Maruyama and Tietze 2012; vander Merwe and Smith 2014). This study confirmed that managers that experience telework do not find decreased productivity from teleworking teams. Question 2 and 8 in the surveys related to how productivity perceptions were affected by telework. When asked about productivity differences with telework (Q2), in S2 87% believed there was no difference. The responses between S1 and S2 showed a statistically significant difference in the responses ($p = 0.0007$) implying that managers had a marked change in beliefs about the productivity of their staff when working from home after they experienced telework, although the question did not measure the direction. Yet the responses to Q8 in both surveys did not differ significantly which means that managers did not change their view that telework would not negatively impact the productivity of the team. Examples of productivity comments from managers show that in some cases productivity increased with telework:

'Some work harder and some are not as productive. The better performing staff find a way to make things work and the poorer performing staff seem content to do less work'; 'I believe that employees tend to be more productive when working from home, however, this depends on the employee and is not a "one size fit all" approach. Some employees need to be actively managed and, in this case, working at the office could mean more productivity';

'My staff in fact have a higher turn-over on producing results since working from home'

'Staff productivity has increased. Getting them to take a break and create work-life balance is a challenge'

Management Trust

Prior studies (Beham et al. 2014; Lebopo et al. 2020; van der Merwe and Smith 2014) have confirmed that management trust has the greatest influence in the successful adoption and implementation of telework in organizations. This study found that experience with telework solidified the already held perception of trust which the managers had prior to lockdown. Over 90% of managers in both surveys stated that their staff could be trusted to telework. No statistically significant difference was found between the S1 and S2 for Q3 and Q4 which addressed trust which managers had in their employees' ability to telework and self-manage when teleworking which implies that managers did not change these views after experiencing telework in their teams. Yet the comments made do not align. Comments were made that there had been a negative stigma around telework and trust had been secured. Yet trust was not universal.

'There was this stigma around whether our young staff would mess around if they were at home. I find (before and after lockdown) that they work diligently when at home, with greater focus at times'; 'It has created a trust relationship between employer and employee. It has given the staff the opportunity to function independently with minimal supervision and to take responsibility for the results'; 'Honestly, the people who actually do work at the office will work at home and people who don't really work at the office won't really work at home'

Preference for Staff to Telework

The results comparing S1 and S2 confirm hypothesis H1 namely that there is a positive change in managers' attitudes towards telework after experiencing the practice. The responses to half of the questions asked in the surveys changed in support of telework after 4 months of telework. This study confirmed the finding in the literature (Silva et al. 2019) that as managers have more experience with telework they are more supportive of the practice. There was a statistically significant change ($p = 0.00004$) in the means of responses to Q10 between S1 and S2 which asked whether managers preferred their staff to work in the office rather than telework. In S1 55% of managers were in favour of working on-site while 40% supported it in S2. Also, when asked in S2 whether their preference for staff to work in the office had changed over the lockdown period (Q16), 47% of the managers agreed with the statement. This positive change in sentiment towards telework demonstrates that once managers experience telework in their teams, they have a more favourable view about the practice. The comments from S2 demonstrate this finding:

> *'The lockdown has had zero impact on our delivery or projects. Telework has showed that staff do not need to be in the office, telework is very possible in (the company) and should be the norm'; 'Some of my managers were certain that some individuals had to work from the office, but this period has shown that it is not true and if managed effectively, they can work from anywhere'; 'Telework is the future. From an organization perspective and from an employee perspective there are advantages and savings for both'*

Table 6. Spearman correlation test result for age

Pair of variables	Spearman rank order correlations (combined data Corrected A) MD pairwise deleted Marked correlations are significant at $p < .05000$			
	Valid N	Spearman R	$t(N - 2)$	p-value
Q16 & AgeQ16 & Age	260	0.162781	2.650000	0.008546
Q10 & Age	461	0.094408	2.031702	0.042759

Table 6 lists the correlation test results that show that age is significantly correlated to the telework preference responses given by the managers. A manager's preference that their staff work from the office increases with the age of the manager. Hence, the moderating effect of age found in literature (Martin and MacDonnell 2012; Tremblay 2002), is confirmed in this study.

Establishing a Telework Practice
Questions 1 and 12 related to how well telework was established in the teams before and after lockdown. The establishment of a telework practice in the organization moved from being voluntary to being mandated by the government because of the lockdown. While this change was forced on the organization and managers had no choice but to allow their staff to work from home, there was a shift in willingness of managers to allow telework and the managers acknowledged that the practice had been embedded in their teams during lockdown. This change was reflected in the statistically significant

difference (p = 0,000017) in the response to Q1 between S1 and S2 which implied that managers believed that telework was more established in their teams after lockdown. In S2, 95% of the managers believed telework had become an established practice in their teams. The managers expressed the following views:

> *'Obviously Covid and Lockdown has accelerated the process and stripped away excuses that made telework impossible before'; 'Lockdown forced telework on the majority of the workforce and in spite of all the challenges it brought about, i.e. juggling between childcare, home-schooling, domestic tasks and work, we can be proud of how well our employees have managed to still keep up with the demand and do not only what is expected, but often above and beyond that. I trust my team to work remotely and would actively encourage it to continue well into the future.'*

Telework Culture

The telework culture in the organization encapsulates several elements. It is the management attitude toward allowing staff to telework; the existence of processes for managing telework; processes for working remotely; and the enablement of staff by providing resources which facilitates telework. The responses of the managers to Q5 regarding the culture of the organization in promoting telework showed a statistically significant difference between surveys (p = 0.045). There was a change from 47% of managers believing that the culture supported telework in S1 to 59% in S2. The change in culture was expressed in the comments:

> *'I am rather shocked at how unprepared the company was for this disaster. We should really prepare better and comprehensively for the future. The future is working from home and working in an agile way. Advice from staff was ignored and opportunities that presented themselves to enable our staff to work from home were not taken up... because senior management felt that employees would take chances'; 'I think covid-19 has accelerated working from home, prior to the pandemic the organisation culture was not one that promoted working from home'.*

Organizational fit for telework has been described in previous studies (Hertel et al. 2005; van der Merwe and Smith 2014). A culture must exist within the organization which encourages telework and supports both managers and teleworkers with processes which enable the practice. A climate of permission must exist within the culture of the organization which then creates trust relationships between managers and teleworkers that supports common working norms. Question 6 addressed the readiness of having such processes. There was no significant statistical difference between responses between S1 and S2 for Q6. The managers mostly believed that the organization lacked adequate processes for managing teleworkers and required new processes appropriate for teleworking staff. The managers had the following comments:

> *'Most managers do not know how to manage teleworkers without micro-managing. There has been an increase in the meetings per day as an attempt to ensure connection but also to drive productivity, this could lead to less productivity'; 'Remote*

working enables productivity to thrive if the correct tools and culture are managed'; 'There is progress in some areas. We need a company-wide approach and processes for telework'

Business Continuity Benefit of Telework

The ability of telework to aid with business continuity is found in prior studies (Green et al. 2017) and also confirmed in this study. Management believed in the ability of telework to make the organization resilient to business interruption. A common view from the managers was that telework processes and a telework culture needed to be matured in the organization to harden it against future disruptions. These were some of the comments:

'Telework allows our organization to be more responsive to things such as disasters'; 'We need to increase capacity to work remotely to adapt to any situation that might arise as with what occurred suddenly with Covid'; 'We have proven that we are resilient and have adapted quickly to ensure continuity and mitigate any risks'

Establishing a Variable and Blended Approach for the Future

What became evident was that managers not only wanted to keep a telework option but were strongly in favour of a blended approach to telework as the work arrangement for the future in the organization. When asked whether telework should be an option for staff after lockdown (Q17) 95% of managers agreed. This finding confirms that managers that have experienced telework in their teams are in favour of embedding the practice as a permanent option for staff. Support for continuing the practice can be seen in comments such as:

'Although was forced upon us (the company) must leverage the opportunity to drive this culture that will mature us for the future of work which is telework'; 'A mobile workforce is truly way to go and it is possible. We just need to get (the company) mindset there so that we can mature as employers and employees in that way'; 'The world has changed - this is an awesome opportunity for the company to save on management costs - outputs should be managed but with the right leadership this kind of working is the way to go'

While most managers supported the continuation of telework as a permanent option in the company, support for a blended approach to telework was stated by many of the managers as can be seen by these comments:

'It's amazing to see that people do actually want to work - the office has far too many distractions. The collaboration at the office is great, but we certainly don't need it every day and a dual approach can work'; 'The nature of the work is such that you do not have to be in the office to get it done. The occasional face to face or meeting might be the only reason to have an office at all. I would be happy working from home 4 days out of 5 and in the office for meeting/s one day as a

catchup'; 'We are all not the same, what works for some may not work for others. So, having a choice to best suits your needs and still meet your productivity targets would be great'

These findings echo recommendations from Bloom (2020) who note that going forward telework should be part-time, optional and a privilege. Also, prior studies have noted that not all jobs fit with telework and a job's characteristics have a significant impact on telework (Lebopo et al. 2020). In the case of this organisation, the IT department has reduced the number of desks by two thirds of pre-lockdown capacity. Staff have been allocated days during which they can be in the office if they would like to be there to accommodate people that want face-to-face interaction. New HR policies to govern remote work arrangements have been introduced and many departments have started to use task completion as a metric to measure productivity since staff are no longer co-located. One outcome of teleworking was the extended hours that staff worked which has led to rules being implemented limiting the number of overtime hours that staff can work.

Summary of Findings

The finding in this study are contextual. The case study is in a financial services organisation that had managed to provide the needed telework resources and capability to its staff for emergency telework. During lockdown the telework practice became established. The findings show that management's preference for telework increased although older managers still had a higher preference for office work. Productivity was found not to reduce with telework and there were anecdotal comments that trust in some employees did increase. It is proposed that these are related factors and explain mechanisms behind the increased telework preference. Going forward, in this organisation the culture changed towards telework during the pandemic and the organisation felt proud that it was able through telework to be more resilient and responsive. Managers were more in favour of making telework a permanent practice for their employees. Having flexible work arrangements was found to be supported by most managers as a permanent option for employees after managers had experienced telework. This finding is found in literature (Silva et al. 2019) and confirmed in this study. Yet there were some concerns. Management processes were still needed to help support telework. Many managers felt that a blended and variable approach would be more appropriate going forward. This meant that employees sometimes needed to be in the office and that certain employees were better suited to telework than others.

5 Conclusion

In times of challenges, telework is a required organisational capability but often managers are reluctant to support it. This study examined whether, after having experience with telework, managers were more in favour of supporting the practice as a work arrangement for employees in their teams. The study found that in the organisation studied, manager support for telework increased and that productivity of some teams improved when teleworking. Further findings were that a telework culture in the organization requires that teleworkers be provided with the necessary resources which includes technology, work processes, and management support in order to succeed. It was also found that managers require different tools and management techniques to manage remote workers. Telework was found to enable business continuity in this case study during a period of business disruption and the positive change in the perception by the managers of the practice helped entrench telework in the organization. This study has limitations. It was limited to one case study. Hence the nature of the organisation impacted the descriptive findings. Comparative studies in various size companies and various industries would add to the findings in this study. Further studies should look at explanatory models and studies that confirm the mechanisms that influence management perceptions, such as productivity and trust.

References

Beham, B., Baierl, A., Poelmans, S.: Managerial telework allowance decisions – a vignette study among German managers. Int. J. Hum. Resour. Manage. **26**, 1385–1406 (2014). https://doi.org/10.1080/09585192.2014.934894

van der Merwe, F.I., Smith, D.C.: Telework. Presented at the Proceedings of the Southern African Institute for Computer Scientist and Information Technologists Annual Conference 2014 on SAICSIT 2014 Empowered by Technology - SAICSIT 2014 (2014). http://dx.doi.org/10.1145/2664591.2664599

Ågerfalk, P.J., Conboy, K., Myers, M.D.: Information systems in the age of pandemics: COVID-19 and beyond. Eur. J. Inf. Syst. **29**, 203–207 (2020). https://doi.org/10.1080/0960085x.2020.1771968

Green, N., Tappin, D., Bentley, T.: Exploring the teleworking experiences of organisations in a post-disaster environment. New Zealand J. Hum. Resour. Manage. 17 (2017)

Martin, B.H., MacDonnell, R.: Is telework effective for organizations? Manag. Res. Rev. **35**, 602–616 (2012). https://doi.org/10.1108/01409171211238820

Silva-C, A., Montoya R, I.A., Valencia A, J.A.: The attitude of managers toward telework, why is it so difficult to adopt it in organizations? Technol. Soc. **59**, 101133 (2019). https://doi.org/10.1016/j.techsoc.2019.04.009

Nakrošienė, A., Bučiūnienė, I., Goštautaitė, B.: Working from home: characteristics and outcomes of telework. Int. J. Manpow. **40**, 87–101 (2019). https://doi.org/10.1108/ijm-07-2017-0172

Greer, T.W., Payne, S.C.: Overcoming telework challenges: outcomes of successful telework strategies. Psychol. Manager J. **17**, 87–111 (2014). https://doi.org/10.1037/mgr0000014

Morikawa, M.: Long commuting time and the benefits of telecommuting. Presented at the RIETI Discussion Paper Series 18-E-025 (2018). https://www.rieti.go.jp/jp/publications/dp/18e025.pdf

Thompson, C.A.: Barriers to the implementation and usage of work–life policies. In: Caligiuri, P., Poelmans, S.A.Y. (eds.) Harmonizing Work, Family, and Personal Life: From Policy to Practice, pp. 209–234. Cambridge University Press, Cambridge (2008)

Collins, A.M., Hislop, D., Cartwright, S.: Social support in the workplace between teleworkers, office-based colleagues and supervisors. N. Technol. Work. Employ. **31**, 161–175 (2016). https://doi.org/10.1111/ntwe.12065

Lebopo, C.M., Seymour, L.F., Knoesen, H.: Explaining factors affecting telework adoption in South African organisations pre-COVID-19. Presented at the Conference of the South African Institute of Computer Scientists and Information Technologists 2020, 11 Sept 2020 (2020). http://dx.doi.org/10.1145/3410886.3410906

Bentley, T., et al.: The Future of Work Program: The Trans-Tasman Telework Survey New Zealand Work Research Institute AUT and IBES (Institute for a Broadband Enabled Society). The University of Melbourne (2013)

Hertel, G., Geister, S., Konradt, U.: Managing virtual teams: a review of current empirical research. Hum. Resour. Manag. Rev. **15**, 69–95 (2005). https://doi.org/10.1016/j.hrmr.2005.01.002

Maruyama, T., Tietze, S.: From anxiety to assurance: concerns and outcomes of telework. Pers. Rev. **41**, 450–469 (2012). https://doi.org/10.1108/00483481211229375

Tremblay, D.G.: Balancing work and family with telework? Organizational issues and challenges for women and managers. Women Manage. Rev. **17**, 157–170 (2002). https://doi.org/10.1108/09649420210425309

Bloom, N.: How working from home works out. Institute for Economic Policy Research (SIEPR). Policy Brief June (2020)

Digital Platforms

Decolonization of Digital Platforms: A Research Agenda for GREAT Domains

Prasanna Karhade[1]([⊠]) [iD], Abhishek Kathuria[2] [iD], Anuttama Dasgupta[3],
Ojaswi Malik[4] [iD], and Benn R. Konsynski[5]

[1] University of Hawai'i at Mānoa, 2404 Maile Way, Honolulu, HI 96822, USA
karhade@hawaii.edu
[2] Indian School of Business, Gachibowli, Hyderabad 500 111, Telangana, India
[3] Indian Institute for Human Settlements, Sadashivanagar, Bengaluru 560 080, India
[4] The University of Hong Kong, K. K. Leung Building, Lung Fu Shan, Hong Kong
[5] Goizueta Business School, Emory University, 1300 Clifton Road, Atlanta, GA 30322, USA

Abstract. Digital platforms are transforming commerce practice. Technology is not separate from the socio-cultural environment in which it is used and, thus, platforms mostly capture and imbue values of their origins in the west. As digital platforms are "migrated" outside the west, western values intrinsically embedded in the digital platforms are also unknowingly imposed around the world. However, research from western, educated, industrialized, rich, and democratic (WEIRD) contexts does not necessarily generalize to the rest of the world. Instead, examining research phenomena on digital platforms anew in growing, rural, eastern, aspirational, transitional (GREAT) contexts is necessary. In this chapter, we highlight the need and pathways for decolonization of digital platforms research in GREAT domains.

Keywords: Digital platforms · Platform strategy · Decolonization of research · India

1 Introduction

1.1 Decolonization of Platform Research

Digital innovations are revolutionizing commerce practice and competitive behaviors of firms across various industries and geographies [1–6]. In particular, digital platforms have grown tremendously with the rise of the internet. Research on platforms has revolved around themes such as network effects, design decisions, and functional- and corporate-level strategies. However, a large proportion of platforms research [7] has arisen from western economies. Technology design is not separate from its socio-cultural environment [8] and, thus, western platforms mostly capture and imbue western values. As these digital platforms are "migrated" or "adopted" outside the US, western values intrinsically embedded in the digital platforms are also unknowingly imposed around the world. However, digital platforms and the accompanying research from western, educated, industrialized, rich, and democratic (WEIRD) contexts do not necessarily

© Springer Nature Switzerland AG 2021
A. Garimella et al. (Eds.): WeB 2020, LNBIP 418, pp. 51–58, 2021.
https://doi.org/10.1007/978-3-030-79454-5_5

generalize to the rest of the world [9]. Instead, examining research phenomena on digital platforms anew in growing, rural, eastern, aspirational, transitional (GREAT) contexts is necessary [10].

Accordingly, we aim to shine a light on the need for the decolonization of digital platforms research in GREAT domains. Sensitizing scholars to the need and pathways for decolonization of research is important [11] and it will enable the transformation of silenced communities and their commerce practices in GREAT domains. We maintain that researching GREAT domains after decolonizing research methods will encourage inclusiveness in research and discourage research colonization. Adopting a ground up approach is essential [11], and thus, embracing data-first inductive-abductive method-ologies [12] can encourage representation of silenced communities and their "native" commerce practices in GREAT domains [13].

1.2 Food Delivery Platforms

We use food delivery platforms as exemplars to aid our discourse on the need for decol-onization of platform research. The food delivery industry around the world has adopted digital platforms to connect multiple user groups including restaurants, customers, finan-cial institutions, and delivery agents. By creating a large, scalable community of inter-connected suppliers and customers, platforms are able to harness positive network effects [14, 15]. Digital platforms largely originated in WEIRD domains, and their migration to GREAT domains has allowed the replication of WEIRD platform design features and values around the world. We are witnessing *scientific colonization*, where only WEIRD questions and norms are understood or appreciated in research [16–18], and GREAT economies merely serve as contextless sources of data for such inquiry [19, 20].

Adoption of food delivery platforms in the GREAT economies like India continues to remain largely non-inclusive and, in fact, excludes a vast proportion of India's diverse population [12]. One reason could arguably be due to the exclusive use of the English language on the platforms which is only spoken by less than 20% of the Indian population. We believe that researchers should broaden their gaze and accordingly, we propose a roadmap for decolonization of platform research in GREAT domains.

2 Digital Platforms in GREAT Domains

2.1 Platform Growth in GREAT Domains

Recent research has examined the complex interaction of multiple factors that influ-ence the participation and non-participation of suppliers (restaurants) on food delivery platforms in GREAT contexts [12]. Investigating the participation of suppliers on the platform is vital for identifying factors that stimulate platform growth in these GREAT domains. By leveraging a research design integrating induction-based analytics with abduction, it was discovered that suppliers that offer medium-priced meals are most likely to participate on food delivery platforms. On the other hand, restaurants at the lower and higher ends of the pricing spectrum are less likely to adopt food delivery platforms. These findings are accompanied with predictors at different levels includ-ing supplier-, institutional-, platform-, competition-, and environmental-level to provide plausible explanations influencing suppliers' decisions to participate on food delivery platforms.

A prominent characteristic of GREAT domains is their incessant growth. The use of technological artifacts such as digital platforms do not follow "rigid scripts" but rather evolve as a fluid, organic growth process [8]. Future research needs to address *how, why and when* growth occurs on various digital platforms in GREAT domains. This inclusive approach to research in GREAT domains will allow representation of different groups by focusing on the growing pains they experience as they use (or refuse) digital platforms.

2.2 Ratings Do not Drive Participation Decisions

Recent studies have focused on examining the impact of online ratings on the restaurant's decision to participate in food delivery platforms in the GREAT economies [10]. Intuitively, it is expected that online ratings should have a bearing on the suppliers' decision to participate in financial transactions on the platform. However, it was found that the customers' ratings do not have a significant impact on restaurants to participate on the food delivery platforms in GREAT domains.

This finding requires a deeper investigation to understand *why* online ratings might not have influenced the suppliers' decision to participate in food delivery. A plausible explanation could be that the restaurant owners think that digital platforms only reached individuals in India who could afford smartphones and speak English. This assumption is limiting as it silences those without access to these privileges. Designers of digital platforms that originate in WEIRD domains need to be cautioned that replicating designs from WEIRD domains and imposing them in GREAT domains will not yield similar outcomes. Hence, future research requires decolonization of digital platforms to heed to diverse groups of populations in GREAT domains.

2.3 Missing Voices on Digital Platforms in GREAT Domains

Studies have also begun to examine the ethical implications of ratings on food delivery platforms. Technological objects can function as knowledge instruments that affect and reflect circles of exclusion in societies that use these technologies [21]. Borrowed from western domains, these online rating systems are designed to hear the voices of only a limited section of society. As online user ratings are voluntary, empirical research methods inadvertently postulate that only data that is available can be counted. This presumption fosters traps of blindness (some relationships are not visible to the researchers) and gullibility (researchers are gullible to see nonexistent relationships in their data) imposed through colonial lenses. Inductive analysis of a prominent Indian food delivery platform revealed that ratings for restaurants in a large number of cities were missing [22]. Moreover, many restaurants that serve alcohol, or that serve meat dishes also lack online ratings. This finding reveals the fallacies of the rating system as the platform was not designed to capture the complexity of the food delivery across the Indian citizenry, especially the *petite bourgeoisie*.

The digital world requires a re-examination of whether it has allowed or silenced those without a voice to communicate freely. It is necessary to question if the rating systems on digital platforms are widening existing circles of exclusion and creating new digital elites. These questions motivate the need for decolonization of research methods and requires a reimagination of ratings systems for GREAT contexts.

2.4 Variety and Authenticity in GREAT Nations

Examining the relationship between restaurant cuisine offerings and consequent user ratings reveals the impact of choice and assortment on supplier performance on digital platforms. Abducting away from patterns induced from data collected from an Indian food delivery platform, unearthed that a variety of restaurants within a given spatial concentration yield high customer ratings [23]. User-generated ratings on the platform can influence other customers' purchasing decisions which can indirectly impact restaurants' performance. Hence, the presence of an assortment of cuisine offerings creates better performance outcomes for restaurants on delivery platforms.

GREAT nations like India are socially and culturally diverse, with embedded norms that influence behaviors [24, 25]. The lack of a pan-India cuisine or a pan-India language reflects this rich diversity inherently embedded in India. These cultural complexities reflect the heterogeneity of the GREAT domains in comparison to the largely homogenous WEIRD world. Hence, predominance of research coming from WEIRD nations like the U.S. is replete with blind-spots bereft of any theoretical and empirical nuances of authenticity and variety. This motivates the need to reinvent the wheel and decolonize research for GREAT domains.

3 Decolonization of Digital Platforms in GREAT Economies

3.1 Decolonization of the Platform

Food delivery platforms function in the public domain and create value by connecting and/or mediating transactions between interdependent user groups. However, the publicly available information from these platforms directly impacts the platform designers or users, as well as indirectly impacts the larger masses. For instance, even users who do not order food online or provide online ratings learn from the information available on these platforms and use it to make their decisions. Hence, these knowledge instruments have the ability to impact societal relations beyond their immediate intended use. By producing knowledge, digital platforms and their encompassed rating systems institute a way of being which require scientific examination to understand their broader implications, especially in GREAT economies.

The power held by digital platforms and online rating systems can be exemplified through the following example. A dissatisfied customer can verbally criticize the restaurant owner in person to bring attention to a problem with their service. Doing so might alert the restaurant at the time, but the lack of public attention does not incentivize them to take actions to resolve the issue. On the other hand, using an online review system on a digital platform to voice concerns attracts attention and directly impacts the restaurant's performance. This makes them highly incentivized to take action to resolve the issue. However, reviews constitute a permanent record of fact which does not change even when corrective action has been taken to address the underlying issue.

Hence, a digitized public domain needs to provide equal access to different sections of society. Structural inequalities embedded in the digital infrastructure of platforms magnifies and institutionalizes the systemic under representation of diverse groups of people. Moreover, platform designs need to flexible and adaptable to changing scenarios. For instance, in the above example if the restaurant takes actions to resolve the problem, they should have the ability to digitally redeem themselves on the platform, akin to the cultural values of forgiveness in eastern domains. Hence, decolonizing the platform is essential to allow different user groups to voice themselves and behavioral changes of suppliers to be reflected on the platform.

3.2 Decolonization of Platform Research

The decolonization of platform research methodologies is essential as WEIRD research cannot be simply imposed onto GREAT domains, as evidenced by prior research [26, 27]. Researchers need to challenge existing power structures and knowledge creation systems by identifying reasons why non-native constructs do not work in GREAT contexts. By asking GREAT questions, scholars can and should reinvent the wheel to yield GREAT answers. We extrapolate on four research and design themes whereby online rating systems on food delivery platforms can be redesigned to be more contextually inclusive and sensitive to GREAT domains.

Adapting Research Frameworks. An important consideration is choosing the right research methodology to explore these new emerging questions. Deductive research designs rely on prior theory which are confirmatory in nature and thus, unable to learn from relationships that emerge from data. Given the relative scarcity of theory native to or appropriately application to GREAT domains, adopting a data-first stance is inevitable. In particular, multi-method research designs that integrate inductive data-driven analytics and abductive discovery can be useful to yield theoretical insights [28] for GREAT domains. Induction allows the discovery of patterns in data [13, 29, 30] which can serve as inputs to the abductive discovery process. By abducting away from the induced patterns, researchers can offer the best plausible explanations to complete the knowledge production process.

Language as a Circle of Exclusion. Using English as the medium of communication on food delivery platforms in GREAT domains creates a circle of exclusion. Not everyone in GREAT domains speaks English, and thus, this choice of language systematically excludes a vast majority of the platform's potential users. Moreover, those with low levels of proficiency with the English language will not be able to express themselves freely and appropriately on these digital platforms. Hence, an essential question platform designers and researchers need to ask is whether the sample of engaged users is representative of the whole population, and accordingly design the platform and research questions to accommodate multiple sections of society. This would also entail consequences arising from reviews in different languages and their comparison by the platform and researchers.

In addition to diversity of languages, GREAT nations like India and Indonesia possess richness in their cuisines. Decolonization of research would require studying the nuances of cuisine variety and assortment in these domains. This cultural richness inspires numerous research questions on authenticity of cuisines and its impact of consumer behaviors.

Access to Resources. Existing circles of exclusion can be easily transformed online to create digital elites and subalterns out of potential users. For instance, not all individuals have access to smartphones, the training to operate smartphones, or access to complementary resources and services (e.g., an email or Facebook account) which automatically excludes them from the platform. Hence, platforms in GREAT domains may consider integrating mechanisms where the oppressed and unheard can be given a voice. Researchers must consider the implications of such exclusions in their research designs. Such circles of exclusion can also inspire new research questions.

To Rate or Not to Rate. Although widely prominent, engagement with the rating systems of digital platforms is not universal. The process of giving reviews can be onerous for non-native English speakers or those with limited internet access. Despite access to resources, some other users may not choose to provide ratings on the digital platform due to collectivistic cultural norms of the GREAT domains. This necessitates platform designers to build instruments that can reduce the burden for those who wish to review and alternatively, gather review related information via access to social networks driven by 'word-of-mouth.' Doing so will make the platform truly representative in the GREAT context in which it is being used. Researchers should also be cognizant of these issues and frame research questions accordingly while striving to identify culturally or contextually appropriate signals or instruments for ratings [15, 31].

4 Conclusion

In this chapter, we have motivated the need to decolonize research on digital platforms that are reshaping commerce practice globally. The technology designs of these platforms imbue the socio-cultural environment of their genesis. As these digital platforms propagate to the rest of the world, western values intrinsically embedded within are also unknowingly imposed. Research inquiry facilitated by these platforms also reflective of western values and contexts [32–34]. However, digital platforms and the accompanying research from western, educated, industrialized, rich, and democratic (WEIRD) contexts do not necessarily generalize to the rest of the world. Instead, examining research phenomena on digital platforms anew in growing, rural, eastern, aspirational, transitional (GREAT) contexts is necessary. Thus, we call for the decolonization of digital platforms and present a research agenda for GREAT domains.

References

1. Karhade, P., Dong, J.Q.: Information technology investment and commercialized innovation performance: dynamic adjustment costs and curvilinear impacts. MIS Q. (2021, forthcoming)
2. Karhade, P., Dong, J.Q.: Innovation outcomes of digitally enabled collaborative problemistic search capability. MIS Q. (2021, forthcoming)

3. Dong, J.Q., Karhade, P., Rai, A., Xu, S.X.: How firms make information technology investment decisions: toward a behavioral agency theory. J. Manage. Inf. Syst. (2021, forthcoming).

4. Dong, J.Q., Karhade, P., Rai, A., Xu, S.X.: Information technology and innovation outputs: the missing link of search evolution. In: Academy of Management Proceedings 2015, vol. 1, p. 13847. Academy of Management Briarcliff Manor, NY (2015)

5. Dong, J.Q., He, J., Karhade, P.: The Penrose effect in resource investment for innovation: evidence from information technology and human capital. ECIS Completed Research 80 (2013)

6. Andrade Rojas, M.G., Kathuria, A., Lee, H.-H.: Attaining operating performance through Pas De Trios of IT, competitive brokerage and innovation. In: Proceedings of the International Conference on Information Systems, Fort Worth (2015)

7. Rietveld, J., Schilling, M.A.: Platform competition: a systematic and interdisciplinary review of the literature. J. Manage. (2021)

8. De Laet, M., Mol, A.: The Zimbabwe bush pump: mechanics of a fluid technology. Soc. Stud. Sci. **30**(2), 225–263 (2000)

9. Henrich, J., Heine, S.J., Norenzayan, A.: Most people are not WEIRD. Nature **466**(7302), 29 (2010)

10. Karhade, P., Kathuria, A.: Missing impact of ratings on platform participation in India: a call for research in GREAT domains. Commun. Assoc. Inf. Syst. **47**(1), 19 (2020)

11. Chilisa, B.: Indigenous Research Methodologies. Sage Publications (2019)

12. Kathuria, A., Karhade, P., Konsynski, B.R.: In the realm of hungry ghosts: multi-level theory for supplier participation on digital platforms. J. Manag. Inf. Syst. **37**(2), 396–430 (2020)

13. Kathuria, A., Karhade, P.P.: You are not you when you are hungry: machine learning investigation of impact of ratings on ratee decision making. In: Xu, J.J., Zhu, B., Liu, X., Shaw, M.J., Zhang, H., Fan, M. (eds.) WEB 2018. LNBIP, vol. 357, pp. 151–161. Springer, Cham (2019). https://doi.org/10.1007/978-3-030-22784-5_15

14. Tiwana, A., Konsynski, B., Bush, A.: Platform evolution: coevolution of platform architecture, governance, and environmental dynamics. Inf. Syst. Res. **21**(4), 675–687 (2010)

15. Kathuria, A., Saldanha, T., Khuntia, J., Andrade Rojas, M., Mithas, S., Hah, H.: Inferring supplier quality in the gig economy: the effectiveness of signals in freelance job markets. In: Proceedings of the 54th Hawaii International Conference on System Sciences, p. 6583, Maui (2021)

16. McIntyre, D.P., Srinivasan, A.: Networks, platforms, and strategy: emerging views and next steps. Strateg. Manag. J. **38**(1), 141–160 (2017)

17. Chen, L., Xu, P., Liu, D.: Effect of crowd voting on participation in crowdsourcing contests. J. Manag. Inf. Syst. **37**(2), 510–535 (2020)

18. Hukal, P., Henfridsson, O., Shaikh, M., Parker, G.: Platform signaling for generating platform content. MIS Q. **44**(3), 1177–1205 (2020)

19. Ramakrishnan, T., Khuntia, J., Kathuria, A., Saldanha, T.J.V.: Business intelligence capabilities. In: Deokar, A.V., Gupta, A., Iyer, L.S., Jones, M.C. (eds.) Analytics and Data Science. AIS, pp. 15–27. Springer, Cham (2018). https://doi.org/10.1007/978-3-319-58097-5_3

20. Andrade Rojas, M., Saldanha, T., Khuntia, J., Kathuria, A., Boh, W.F.: Overcoming innovation deficiencies in mexico: use of open innovation through it and closed innovation through IT by small and medium enterprises. In: Proceedings of the 54th Hawaii International Conference on System Sciences, p. 617, Kauai (2021)

21. Akrich, M.: The Description of Technical Objects, pp. 205–224 (1992)

22. Dasgupta, A., Karhade, P., Kathuria, A., Konsynski, B.: Holding space for voices that do not speak: design reform of rating systems for platforms in GREAT economies. In: Proceedings of the 54th Hawaii International Conference on System Sciences, p. 2564, Maui (2021)

23. Karhade, P., Kathuria, A., Konsynski, B.: When choice matters: assortment and participation for performance on digital platforms. In: Proceedings of the 54th Hawaii International Conference on System Sciences, p. 1799, Maui (2021)
24. Khuntia, J., Saldanha, T., Kathuria, A.: Dancing in the tigers' den: MNCs versus local firms leveraging IT-enabled strategic flexibility. In: Proceedings of the International Conference on Information Systems, Auckland (2014)
25. Kathuria, A., Khuntia, J., Karhade, P., Ning, X.: Don't ever take sides with anyone against the family: family ownership and information management. In: Proceedings of the Americas Conference on Information Systems, Cancun (2019)
26. Ning, X., Khuntia, J., Kathuria, A., Karhade, P.: Information technology investment, environmental hostility, and firm performance: the roles of family ownership in an emerging economy. In: Proceedings of the 53rd Hawaii International Conference on System Sciences, Maui (2020)
27. Ning, X., Khuntia, J., Kathuria, A., Karhade, P.: Ownership and management control effects on IT investments: a study of indian family firms. In: Proceedings of the International Conference on Information Systems, Hyderabad (2020)
28. Karhade, P., Shaw, M.J., Subramanyam, R.: Patterns in information systems portfolio prioritization. MIS Q. 39(2), 413–434 (2015)
29. Karhade, P.: IT portfolio management: an enterprise risk management-based perspective. In: AMCIS 2007 Proceedings, p. 405 (2007)
30. Karhade, P., Shaw, M.: Rejection and selection decisions in the IT portfolio composition process: an enterprise risk management based perspective. In: AMCIS 2007 Proceedings, p. 221 (2007)
31. Kathuria, A., Saldanha, T., Khuntia, J., Andrade Rojas, M.G., Hah, H.: Strategic intent, contract duration, and performance: evidence from micro-outsourcing. In: Proceedings of the International Conference on Information Systems, Fort Worth (2015)
32. Saldanha, T.J.V., Kathuria, A., Khuntia, J., Konsynski, B., Andrade Rojas, M.: Leveraging digitalization of services for performance: evidence from the credit union industry. In: Proceedings of the International Conference on Information Systems, Seoul (2017)
33. Saldanha, T., Kathuria, A., Khuntia, J., Konsynski, B.: Ghosts in the machine: how marketing and human capital investments enhance customer growth when innovative services leverage self-service technologies. Inf. Syst. Res. (2021, forthcoming).
34. Vitzthum, S., Kathuria, A., Konsynski, B.: Toys become tools: from virtual worlds to real commerce. Commun. Assoc. Inf. Syst. 29 (2011)

The Mechanics of the Gig Economy: A System Dynamics Approach

Jae Choi[1]([✉]), Derek L. Nazareth[2], and Thomas Ngo-Ye[3]

[1] Pittsburg State University, 1701 S. Broadway, Pittsburg, KS 66762, USA
`jchoi@pittstate.edu`
[2] University of Wisconsin-Milwaukee, P.O. Box 742, Milwaukee, WI 53201, USA
`derek@uwm.edu`
[3] Alabama State University, 915 S. Jackson Street, Montgomery, AL 36104, USA
`tngoye@alasu.edu`

Abstract. As organizations look to become leaner, more workers find themselves in the role of an independent contractor participating in the gig economy. This research describes the creation of a design science artifact that captures dynamic and systemic relations between the conventional and gig economy. Considering the gig economy's disruptive impact on the labor market, this research focuses on the role of platform effectiveness and relative pricing in on the dual economies. It seeks to contribute to the extant literature by capturing the complex and dynamic aspects of the two parallel economies. Ongoing work and future plans are outlined and formulated.

Keywords: Online platform economy · Gig economy · Labor market · System dynamics · Simulation

1 Introduction

Over the last decade, the gig economy has become increasingly significant in the labor marketplace. Estimates indicate independent workers comprise up to 20% of the paid workforce in some countries [9] and 16% in USA [20]. This disruption to the traditional workforce is enabled by the availability of online platforms that connect customers to providers. The attraction of being one's own boss, and settings one's own hours has allowed competent service providers to remove themselves from the traditional workforce and pick and choose assignments as freelancers. What originally began as a small coterie of marketplaces connecting independent sellers to buyers of physical goods has morphed into a wide range of online platforms spanning multiple sectors including transport (delivery, moving), personal service (dog walking, repairs, babysitting, home healthcare), and selling (trading physical goods) [4]. In this research, we treat the gig economy as distinct from the sharing economy in that the former focuses on services, while the latter includes assets like apartments, rooms, parking spaces, storage space, automobiles, etc. The transition to the gig economy is not without risk, though. Participants give up corporate benefits and need to plan for the uncertainty of future work.

© Springer Nature Switzerland AG 2021
A. Garimella et al. (Eds.): WeB 2020, LNBIP 418, pp. 59–66, 2021.
https://doi.org/10.1007/978-3-030-79454-5_6

However, nimble participants have adapted to take on a variety of jobs to fill the gaps between steady assignments. Motivations for entering the gig economy vary, including autonomy, work-life balance, extra earnings, working between jobs, and the only available option in some cases. Gig workers are classified as free agents, reluctants, casual earners, and financially strapped, based upon their choice and need for income [9].

Some advocates of the gig economy have made sweeping claims about the end to traditional employment, and a shift to a predatory platform driven paradigm. This shift has not come to pass in that the gig economy still represents a small part of the labor economy. More recently, the literature has recognized this as a labor issue that raises challenging questions [18]. One of the key questions that arises is whether online platforms are distinct from conventional work in the labor market. It has been suggested that there is need for research on the systemic relationship between the conventional and gig economies [18]. Given the prevailing organizational, environmental, and contextual factors, this proves to be a challenging area, in light of the complexity and dynamism of the problem domain. Disruptions in the labor market can be triggered by a variety of phenomena, including economic crises, natural disasters, sustained climate issues, military strife, and more recently, the Covid-19 pandemic. Interestingly, the pandemic has forced many traditional workers to adopt the work patterns of providers in the gig economy.

In an effort to better understand the effect of the gig economy, this research utilizes the design science methodology [6], which seeks to create artifacts that are intended to address specific organizational problems and provide rigorous evaluation of these artifacts based on utility rather than an empirical test of theories.

Following the design science process outlined in [13], this paper presents the initial steps taken in developing an artifact that captures dynamic and systemic relation between the conventional and gig economies. The paper is organized as follows. A review of the extant literature pertaining to gig economy and enabling online platforms serves as the foundation for building the model and is presented in the next section. Objectives for a model that will shed light on the implications of the gig economy are then addressed. A dynamic model of the constructs underlying the gig economy and its associated labor market is then assembled and presented. Ongoing work and future plans are formulated and discussed.

2   Prior Studies and Problem Characteristics

The gig economy has been defined as people using platforms to sell their labor [17]. Studies have identified several distinctive types of platforms. Some researchers have categorized them based on their objectives, including platforms for platforms, platforms for digital tools, platforms mediating work, retail platforms, and service-providing platforms [8]. Others have focused on the role of individuals in the platform, identifying platform architects, cloud-based consultants, freelancers, service providers, workers involved in online micro-tasking, content producers, and social media influencers [18].

Some studies have adopted a more utopian perspective, emphasizing the ability of peer-to-peer connections to erode the dominance of the conventional corporate model [3]; the monetization of assets through sharing platforms to reduce dependency on labor income [16]; reduced transaction cost through crowd-source ratings and reputational information [16]; or an emerging networked society of microentrepreneurs where workers are afforded the flexibility and choice that is generally available to nonprofessionals in conventional jobs [14, 16].

Others adopt a more dystopian view, focusing on workforce control though information technologies and related algorithms. These researchers have focused on technology's role in surveillance [21], the usage of people analytics in corporate human resource management [2], unfair outcomes in evaluation and ranking systems, disproportionally affecting race and gender [10], and developments in undermining transparency [12], among others.

The reality lies somewhere in between. Kalleberg [7] suggested that the growth of "market-mediated, open employment relationships" entails the replacement of administrative rules with market mechanisms for determining job outcomes. Further, he argued that it shifts economic risks and responsibility for skill development onto workers while firms are no longer willing to provide training for their workforce. Market-mediated open employment relationships have been seen as enabling a new wave of online outsourcing in low and middle-income countries. It is posited this is due to workers not having the opportunity to benefit from closed employment relationships and be granted certain legal rights and guarantees over labor conditions [19]. Eventually, researchers sought to investigate the notion of job quality employing multiple dimensions in market-mediated, open employment relationships to highlight the attractive features of gig jobs in comparison to traditional ones. Some studies adopted a multi-pronged approach to identify characteristics and mechanisms in platform-enabled gig jobs. In addition, they also explored the causes of lower income (e.g. the high ratio of unpaid work to paid labor, unavailability of work), issues involving lack of employment-linked social security, worker's control at the place of work, or higher uncertainty relevant to gig jobs [1].

3 Solution Characteristics and Design Methodology

The design science process includes successive tasks of problem identification, objective formulation, design and development, demonstration, evaluation, and communication [13]. The prior section identified the problem, and this section is devoted to specifying the objectives for the artifact. Understanding the effects of the gig economy requires a systematic exploration of its impacts under a variety of conditions. The complexity of labor markets and the dynamic nature of platform phenomenon make it difficult to assess the implications of gig job characteristics, and to determine which set of parameters would lead to more efficient labor markets. Attempting to explore the impact of different gig job characteristics in a real-world setting would require a large number of field experiments. In an attempt to understand the gig economy more effectively, this research adopts a simulation-based approach that permits controlled manipulation of the relevant constructs.

The predictive capability of the model represents one of the foremost objectives in this research. The ability to examine the impact of alternative options under various environmental and organizational conditions provides managers with guidance when making the decisions central to the gig economy and workforce outsourcing. Additionally, the solution approach must adequately represent the real-world phenomenon, be robust, and reliable. The artifact in this research is a system dynamics model that allows decision makers to evaluate the impact of alternative human resource decisions under varying environmental and industry conditions.

This use of a system dynamics model permits the investigation of the effects of different decisions and environmental conditions on an organization's workforce. System dynamics uses a combination of first order linear and non-linear difference equations to relate qualitative and quantitative factors within and across time periods [15] and is based on principles developed by Forrester to study managerial and dynamic decisions using control principles [5]. System dynamics was chosen for the simulation as it permits examination of the relationships between constructs within a time period, as well as across time periods. System dynamics models comprise stocks, flows, converters, and connectors. Stocks represent organizational resources that can accumulate or deplete over time. Stocks are connected by flows, which increase or deplete the stock levels, through resource utilization and replenishment. Stocks and flows are governed by conserving laws, which ensure that future stock levels are based on current levels, moderated by all flows. In contrast to stocks, converters hold inputs, outputs, and intermediate values and do not accumulate values. Converters are linked to other constructs using connectors. Positive or self-reinforcing and negative or self-correcting feedback loops play an important role in determining dynamic behavior because most complex behaviors usually arise from feedback among the system components, not from the complexity of the components [15].

4   Design of the Gig Economy Model

The model seeks to capture the relationships in the labor market when some of its work is outsourced through online platforms, and represents the third step in the design science process. The foremost decision to be made is the unit of analysis for the model. Several options are available, including modeling at the level of the gig economy worker, the platform, the industry, or the national labor market. Model constructs and their relationships will differ, depending on the level selected. In this case, we elect to study the phenomenon at the industry level. Models at the individual and platform levels are less likely to be generalizable, while the entire labor market will entail wide disparity in constituent industries. Estimates of gig work in USA range from 38% in recreation to 2% in manufacturing [20]. In addition, modeling at an industry level would facilitate greater insights. When assembling a system dynamics model, the construction and validation procedures are closely interwoven. Creating the model requires the identification of stocks, converters, flows, and connectors that are intrinsic to the model. Textual analysis of published academic and professional literature facilitates the initial identification of these concepts. The process is repeated, and the model evolves iteratively. Much of the art of system dynamics modeling is discovering and representing the feedback processes. Application of these principles to the gig economy at the industry context results in the causal model depicted in Fig. 1.

The key constructs in the model are companies and individuals that participate in the gig economy, and the price of the gig projects relative to traditional workers. The number

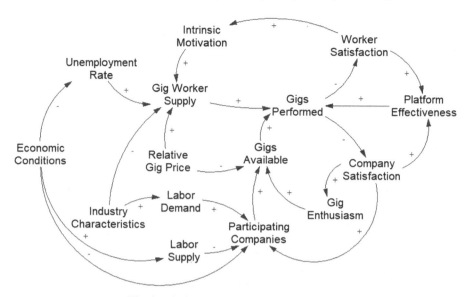

Fig. 1. Platform-enabled gig economy model

of companies participating in the gig economy is shaped by the demand and supply of labor, moderated by prevailing economic conditions. While it is generally accepted that gig worker wages will be lower than traditional workers, companies that are squeezed financially may opt for more gig work. In contrast, some industries may preclude significant gig work, due to regulations, confidentiality, liability considerations, and client preferences. A combination of environmental conditions and industry characteristics will shape the precursors to the number of companies participating. Also of importance is the degree of familiarity and enthusiasm associated with outsourcing gig work by the company. Not all companies within an industry will have the same enthusiasm for participation. These two constructs will shape the number of gig opportunities available. Another segment of the model deals with the gig workers. The motivation for gig work includes work autonomy, work-life balance, extra earnings, working between jobs, and the lack of other options. Coupled with the prevailing unemployment rate, this will shape the number of workers seeking to enter the gig economy. A crucial part of the model is the relative price of gig work. This affects the number of gig jobs, as well as the number of gig workers. Lower rates will boost the number of jobs, while depressing the number of workers. Estimates for short term gig worker pay hover around 40% of traditional workers, while experienced and skilled individuals hired as contractors may earn comparable or greater paychecks than employees. However, in both cases, the overall cost to the company is lowered since benefits and other expenses associated with full-time employees are obviated. The last segment of the model relates to platform effectiveness. Without an efficient and competent platform, matching between gig workers and opportunities will be problematic. Satisfaction with the gig experience for the worker as well as the company forms the basis for feedback loops in the model.

A critical aspect of the model is the presence of feedback loops. In this case, there are loops that address gig worker availability, company participation, and platform effectiveness. All these loops are balancing loops, ensuring that the model will not display unfettered growth or decline.

5   Future Research

5.1   Model Development and Validation

While the causal diagram provides a sense of how constructs in the gig economy are related, the real utility is manifest when it is transformed into a working model. This represents the next step in the research, and entails describing detailed relationships between the causal links. Model equations are assembled in parameterized form, so as to permit exploration of a number of scenarios and generate results that are not restricted to a specific organizational context. Difference equations in the relationships are incorporated to ensure that the model adequately reflects reality. Equations will be assembled based upon findings from published literature.

Validation of the model represents an integral part of its construction. Validation is accomplished on two distinct dimensions. Structural validation of the model seeks to determine if it reflects the real world accurately, while behavioral assessment focuses on the model behavior during execution and assesses the degree of confidence that can be placed in the results. Structural validation involves tasks of boundary adequacy, structure verification, parameter verification, dimensional consistency, and extreme condition analysis [11]. These tasks serve to ensure that relevant constructs are included in the model, the structure represents relationships from the real world, the parameters and dimensions are consistent with traditional notions, and that the model is robust under a variety of conditions.

Validation of individual equations is easily accomplished through suitable calibration and methodical assessment of the response under all valid combinations of inputs. However, validation of the entire model is considerably more complex, and correct functioning of individual equations does not guarantee adequate performance of the model. Once again, an iterative process is adopted. Testing the model in a variety of organizational and environmental conditions allows for systematic exploration of the model behavior. Some of the behavioral assessment is aimed at ensuring that basic system dynamic principles are not violated, e.g. stock values do not go negative. Other aspects deal with behavior patterns. The working model will include loops, and any reinforcing loops need to be checked for rapid trends towards zero or unacceptably high values. Similarly, in a balancing loop, it is necessary to verify that there are no unacceptable oscillations, and that any oscillations are suitably damped. Finally, the model is checked for behavior patterns that are consistent to the real world, examining trends and how quickly a variable achieves stability, rather than focusing on specific values generated through the simulation. Recalibration of the model equations and parameters facilitates the construction of a more accurate and robust model.

5.2 Application to Real-World Cases

The next two steps of the design science process are accomplished through application to real-world cases. This involves setting the context and the scope of the application. The scope could be regional, national, or global. The context specifies whether the application is limited to one platform, an entire industry, or all industries. The larger the scope and the wider the context, the less precise the model will be. Narrow scopes and limited contexts offer restricted insights and fewer opportunities to generalize the findings. Regardless of the scope and context selected, the model needs to be calibrated suitably. Aside from the overall magnitude of the numbers involved, the perceived attractiveness for workers and the relative substitutability for organizations will also need to be adjusted. Our preference is to run the model for a specific industry at a national level. The model would not consider work performed by overseas providers, since that involves foreign transaction as well as legal ramifications.

Running the model requires a systematic exploration of the problem space, by varying individual inputs in a controlled manner. In addition to examining the effect of specific inputs, e.g. various price points for gig work, we also plan to examine the effect of different environmental conditions, e.g. stagnant, contracting, or growing economies. This would offer deeper and broader insights into the gig economy within the selected industry.

6 Conclusions

The concept of freelance work has long predated the gig economy – substitute teachers, float nurses, are well-established examples. However, the gig economy made these exchange opportunities more efficient. While the gig economy has made some inroads into the traditional labor markets, it is unclear if it will play a sizeable role in the future. Nevertheless, it is here to stay. This research seeks to understand the mechanics of gig economy. The initial steps towards formulating a causal diagram in system dynamics are described, and subsequent development of the model is outlined. The current work and subsequent steps will contribute to knowledge on the gig economy, capturing the dynamic interplay of the labor market in the gig and traditional economies.

References

1. Berg, J.: Income security in the on-demand economy: findings and policy lessons from a survey of crowdworkers. Comp. Lab. L. Pol'y J. **37**(3), 543–569 (2016)
2. Bodie, M.T., Cherry, M.A., McCormick, M.L., Tang, J.: The law and policy of people analytics. Univ. Colorado Law Rev. **88**, 961–1042 (2017)
3. Einav, L., Farronato, C., Levin, J.: Peer-to-peer markets. Ann. Rev. Econ. **8**(1), 615–635 (2016)
4. Farrell, D., Greig, F., Hamoudi, A.: The Online Platform Economy in 2018: Drivers, Workers, Sellers, and Lessors. JPMorgan Chase (2018)
5. Forrester, J.W.: Industrial Dynamics. MIT Press, Cambridge, MA (1961)
6. Hevner, A.R., March, S.T., Park, J., Ram, S.: Design science in information systems research. MIS Q. **28**(1), 75–105 (2004)

 7. Kalleberg, A.L.: Good jobs, bad jobs: the rise of polarized and precarious employment systems in the United States, 1970s–2000s, Russell Sage Foundation (2011)
 8. Kenney, M., Zysman, J.: The rise of the platform economy. Issues Sci. Technol. **32**(3), 61–69 (2016)
 9. McKinsey Global Institute: Independent work: Choice, necessity, and the gig economy (2016)
10. Noble, S.U.: Algorithms of Oppression: How Search Engines Reinforce Racism. NYU Press, New York (2018)
11. Qudrat-Ullah, H.: Structural validation of system dynamics and agent-based simulation models. In: 19th European Conference on Modelling and Simulation ECMS 2005, Riga, Latvia (2005)
12. Pasquale, F.: The Black Box Society. Harvard University Press, Cambridge (2015)
13. Peffers, K., Tuunanen, T., Rothenberger, M.A., Chatterjee, S.: A design science research methodology for information systems research. J. Manag. Inf. Syst. **24**(3), 45–77 (2007)
14. Schor, J.B., Attwood-Charles, W., Cansoy, M., Ladegaard, I., Wengronowitz, R.: Dependence and precarity in the sharing economy. Unpublished paper, Boston College (2017)
15. Sterman, J.:. Business Dynamics: Systems Thinking and Modeling for a Complex World. Irwin/McGraw-Hill, New York (2010)
16. Sundararajan, A.: The Sharing Economy: The End of Employment and the Rise of Crowd-Based Capitalism. MIT Press, Boston (2016)
17. Taylor, M., Marsh, G., Nicol, D., Broadbent, P.: Good Work: The Taylor Review of Modern Working Practices. UK Crown Press (2017)
18. Vallas, S., Schor, J.B.: What do platforms do? Understanding the gig economy. Ann. Rev. Sociol. **46**, 273–294 (2020)
19. Webster, E., Lambert, R., Beziudenhout, A.: Grounding Globalization: Labour in the Age of Insecurity. Blackwell Publishing, Malden (2008)
20. Yildirmaz, A., Goldar, M., Klein, S.: Illuminating the Shadow Workforce: Insights into the Gig Economy for the Enterprise. ADP Research Institute (2020)
21. Zuboff, S.: Surveillance capitalism. Esprit **5**(1), 63–77 (2019)

Digital Platforms and Infobesity: A Research Agenda

Prasanna Karhade[1]($\boxtimes$) (ID), Abhishek Kathuria[2] (ID), Ojaswi Malik[3] (ID),
and Benn Konsynski[4]

[1] University of Hawai'i at Mānoa, 2404 Maile Way, Honolulu, HI 96822, USA
karhade@hawaii.edu
[2] Indian School of Business, Gachibowli, Hyderabad 500 111, Telangana, India
[3] The University of Hong Kong, K. K. Leung Building, Lung Fu Shan, Hong Kong
[4] Goizueta Business School, Emory University, 1300 Clifton Road, Atlanta, GA 30322, USA

Abstract. Digital platforms are transforming commerce practice in a variety of industries. Driven by network effects, platforms are incentivized to increase supplier and consumer participation. Increased participation on digital platforms can give rise to infobesity, a condition characterized by information overload whereby various stakeholders collect and are required to process vast amount of information. The causes and consequences of platform-induced infobesity need to be further examined. Accordingly, we develop a research agenda at the intersection of digital platform strategy and infobesity.

Keywords: Digital platforms · Infobesity · Information overload · Supplier participation · Online reviews

1 Introduction

Digital innovation is transforming commerce practice and competition in a variety of industries [1–8]. Digital platforms in particular are connecting at least two large groups of interdependent users in the market, namely suppliers and customers [9]. By creating a large, scalable community of inter-connected suppliers and customers, platforms can harness the benefits of network effects [10]. A given customer is likely to derive more value from being present of a platform, if there are a greater number of suppliers as well as customers present on the platform. For instance, a customer using a food delivery platform such as Food Panda would prefer to choose from a variety of products (meals, snacks and drinks) offered by a large network of suppliers (restaurants). Moreover, they would derive greater value from the platform if there is also a large network of customers who have written reviews for different suppliers (restaurants). Network effects largely dictate digital platform strategy whereby platforms are incentivized to increase participation and network size of both suppliers and customers. However, in doing so digital platforms generate *infobesity* – a condition of information overload characterized by an abundance of information which can adversely affect decision-making, productivity, and the morale of various stakeholders. Infobesity on digital platforms can affect many

© Springer Nature Switzerland AG 2021
A. Garimella et al. (Eds.): WeB 2020, LNBIP 418, pp. 67–74, 2021.
https://doi.org/10.1007/978-3-030-79454-5_7

stakeholders including the platform-designer, the user groups such as the suppliers and customers, as well as other indirect stakeholders such as policy makers. For instance, in the food delivery example above, a large variety of restaurant and cuisine choices can overwhelm consumers and prevent them from making well-informed decisions by increasing their cognitive load [11].

While network effects (indirectly) push platforms to increase infobesity, there is a need to study sources of platform-induced infobesity as well as its consequences for the platform and its various stakeholders. Accordingly, in this chapter, we map out a research agenda at the intersection of digital platform strategy and infobesity.

2   Platforms and Infobesity

2.1   Food Delivery Platforms

Digital innovation and platforms in particular have transformed a multitude of industries such as software development, payments, labor markets, ride sharing, and food delivery [12–14]. This chapter focuses on the dynamics within food delivery platforms [11, 15–17], to explore the sources and consequences of infobesity within digital platforms. Food delivery platforms have monetized the digitization of ubiquitous, reoccurring, and low-value transactions. As food is a basic necessity of life, food delivery platforms can serve large potential markets and can offer opportunities for transactions that are of small value yet are novel. However, such platforms are non-exclusive with minimal ability to lock-in users due to low multi-homing costs. Hence, food delivery platforms continue to attract large investments but have only delivered an elusive serving of profitability.

2.2   Infobesity and Food Delivery Platforms

Food delivery platforms are multi-sided as they connect multiple user groups including suppliers (restaurants), consumers, financial institutions, and delivery agents. Interdependent forces involving each of these user groups increase infobesity not only for these stakeholders but also for the platform providers.

Platform Designers. A platform not only offers a food delivery service, but also a food discovery service through ratings and reviews. Hence, owners and designers of the platform would want more restaurants to participate on their platform as a larger variety of offerings in terms of cuisines, locations, or price ranges is likely to attract a greater number of customers to the platform. Simultaneously, platform designers also want more customers using their service and to record more reviews which would inform and ultimately attract other customers to the platform. Moreover, more customers on the platform, in turn would also encourage more restaurants to join the platform. This would ultimately create a virtuous loop. However, increased number of users on the platform can also flood the platform with excessive amounts of data creating infobesity which can create hinderances in the management of the platform.

Restaurants. Restaurants on the platform not only produce the core product (food that is to be delivered), but also advertise on the platform. Presence on the platform is likely to encourage these suppliers to increase their cuisine offerings in order to be more competitive. Moreover, they would want to amp up their marketing efforts in order to increase their visibility among consumers. These activities increase infobesity and can derail restaurants from their core strategy and ultimately have a negative impact on their business. In particular, while joining the platform may increase demand for restaurants, it is also accompanied with a lot of demand uncertainty. Exposure to volatile demands increases the risk that the restaurant may not be able to meet the volatile demand, thereby negatively impacting their ratings on the platform, and eventually their sales [15].

Customers. Customers generate demand for the food produced by restaurants, and also create valuable content by rating and reviewing restaurants. However, many consumers face the problem of plenty leaving them overwhelmed while choosing a delivery option. While wanting to provide a range of offerings, platform can over burden the customer with boundless cuisines as well as limitless ratings for different restaurants creating the problem of infobesity [11]. Inundated with information, customers are likely to be left frustrated which can even affect their choice to even participate on the platform.

Delivery Agents. Delivery agents connect the suppliers and customers by physically delivering food orders. Increased presence of both suppliers and customers can burden these agents with excess work and information which can impact their performance.

3   Old Findings Motivate New Questions

In this section we elaborate on few exemplar recent papers researching participation on digital platforms. The findings from these exemplars allow us to formulate new emerging research questions at the intersection of digital platform strategy and infobesity.

3.1   Supplier Participation on Digital Platforms

Recent literature has examined the complex interaction of multiple factors influencing the participation and non-participation of restaurants on food delivery platforms [15]. By leveraging a research design integrating induction-based analytics with abduction, prior research has discovered that restaurants that offer medium-priced meals are most likely to participate on such platforms. On the other hand, restaurants at the lower and higher ends of the pricing spectrum are less likely to create a presence on delivery platforms. These findings are accompanied with predictors at different levels including supplier-, institutional-, platform-, competition-, and environmental-level to provide plausible explanations of mechanisms influencing suppliers' decisions to participate on food delivery platforms.

The finding that a large number of restaurants do not participate on the platform motivates us to ask new questions. Is it possible that the mere presence of a large number of suppliers on the platform creates infobesity for new entrants and reduces their participation incentives? Furthermore, it is indeed plausible that competing in platforms demonstrating high levels of infobesity is likely to be less profitable. Platforms with a large number of restaurants are likely to face greater competition which instigates the fear of new restaurants losing their identity while competing with many other. Moreover, in order to attract higher reviews from customers, these restaurants might also be coerced to increase their marketing expense which motivates research to understand the relationship between infobesity and supplier surplus on digital platforms.

3.2 Missing Ratings and the GREAT Context

Research conducted on digital platforms in western, educated, industrialized, rich, and democratic (WEIRD) contexts cannot be generalized to the rest of the world. Instead, examining all research phenomena anew in Growing, Rural, Eastern, Aspirational, Transitional (GREAT) contexts is gaining traction recently [16]. Recent studies have focused on examining the impact of online ratings on ratees' decision to participate in digital platforms in GREAT economies. It was found that these ratings do not have a significant impact on restaurants to participate on the food delivery platforms in GREAT domains.

Future research needs to carefully examine whether the impact of infobesity in digital platforms is exacerbated in GREAT domains. GREAT economies such as India, Indonesia, and other South East Asian nations account for a significant proportion of the world population and economic output. The information environment in these domains is extremely rich owing to its evolving and aspirational nature [18–21]. Dispersed with rural services undergoing a transition into urban offerings, these economies significantly differ from those in WEIRD domains. Hence, a plausible explanation to the missing impact of ratings in GREAT contexts could be owing to the presence of high levels of infobesity. The presence of copious amounts of information in these evolving domains, does not motivate the need for additional information on the platforms. In practice, while navigating through the vast multitude of choices or existing reviews on the platform, customers are likely to face increased cognitive overload. This creates infobesity and can deter them from adding new reviews, thereby preventing them from voicing their opinions. This could lead to a systematic under-representation of diverse groups of populations on digital platforms in GREAT nations [17].

3.3 Impact of Variety on Restaurant Performance

The performance of suppliers on food delivery platforms can be adjudicated by the ratings provided by customers. User-generated ratings on the platform can influence other customers' purchasing decisions which ultimately impacts restaurants' performance. Abducting away from induced patterns from analyzing data in a recent study revealed that a variety of restaurants within a given spatial concentration yield high ratings by customers [11]. Furthermore, restaurants offering varied cuisines also attract high ratings. Hence, the presence of an assortment of offerings creates better performance outcomes for restaurants on delivery platforms.

However, this finding requires further probing in identifying the limit at which restaurant and cuisine variety creates infobesity. While the number of restaurants and variety in cuisines may have a positive impact on ratings, it is essential for researchers to find how these factors individually or collectively influence infobesity.

4   New Questions on Infobesity

In this chapter, we aim to go beyond recent papers and define an agenda for future research. As digital platforms continue to grow, it also gives rise to infobesity and the problem of plenty which can undermine the platforms' performance. We shine the light on two broad questions at the intersection of digital platform strategy and infobesity that go beyond the narrative in the extant literature [22]. We call for research to explore (1) the predictors of infobesity on digital platforms and (2) the consequences of infobesity on platform performance.

The first question is necessary to discover the sources of infobesity that platforms need to manage, and the varying impact of different contributors to infobesity. The constant proliferation of digital platforms continues to metamorphosize traditional management practices. The notion of convenience on platforms has reduced the distance between customers and suppliers, while also offering new-age customer experiences and supplier functionalities [23]. These enhanced capabilities on digital platforms create additional sources of information which can be sources or predictors of unintended infobesity. For instance, the platform designers of food delivery platforms, have access to real-time data such as the time the customer placed the order, or the time the delivery agent delivered the order to the customer. Additional data points include location-based data such as the GPS-tracked location of delivery agents along the way. At the same time, customers are exposed to constant notifications from these digital platform applications. Hence, there is a need for future research to explore the different sources of infobesity and degree and frequency with which these information sources influence different user groups of the digital platform.

It also essential to study the consequences of infobesity on platforms. This includes both direct and indirect effects of infobesity on the different stakeholders such as the suppliers, the customers, the platform designers, and others such as delivery agents. Understanding the relationship between infobesity and supplier performance can have rich managerial implications for the platform designers such as determining how they can increase supplier participation. Furthermore, exploring the underlying effects of infobesity on customers' decision-making can aid platforms in identifying the right incentives for customers to submit more reviews and be heard.

An additional important consideration is choosing the right research methodology to explore these new emerging questions. Since strong theory is not yet available on these emerging sources of infobesity, multi-method research designs that integrate inductive data-driven analytics and abductive discovery can be useful to yield theoretical insights [24]. Induction allows the discovery of patterns in data [25–27] which can serve as inputs to the abductive discovery process. By abducting away from the induced patterns, researchers can offer the best plausible explanations to complete the knowledge production process.

5   Implications for Platform Designers

Platform designers control and shape the interface for all user groups and hence their design choices directly dictate the infobesity experienced on the platform [28]. Every feature added to the platform has an information footprint and thus influences (i.e., increases or decreases) infobesity. Thus, introduction of new features on digital platforms on a continual basis correspondingly should make managing infobesity an ongoing design challenge for platform designers.

On the one hand, platform designers want to unleash the benefits of network effects resulting from large user networks [29]. On the other hand, the detrimental effects of infobesity should motivate platform designers to establish explicit design guidelines for reducing the cognitive load of platform users. Hence, platform designers are required to continuously manage the tradeoffs between choosing an information rich interface versus providing the same (or similar) information while explicitly taking steps to reduce the cognitive load on their consumers.

In particular, food delivery platform designers can provide a greater selection of restaurants for customers to choose from. Or these designers can take a deeper dive to show a variety of cuisines at relatively few restaurants for their customers. The tradeoffs involved in listing a larger number of restaurants versus showing a lot of cuisine variety at a smaller number of restaurants need to be explored. In summary, platform designers need to be aware that their design choices in depicting restaurants and cuisines on food delivery platforms directly influence the customers' information or infobesity experience and ultimately influence their consumers' choice or participating on the platform.

6   Conclusion

The proliferation of participation on digital platforms has given rise to infobesity that requires careful examination. In this chapter, we develop a research agenda at the intersection of digital platform strategy and infobesity. We draw on past research findings to motivate new questions that deal with the sources and consequences of infobesity within food delivery platforms. Questions pertaining to sources of infobesity such as; implications of high supplier presence and impact of different social contexts on infobesity are elaborated upon. We also provide a framework to approach future research on understanding the consequences of infobesity on different direct and indirect stakeholders. Moreover, we put forward the use of multi-method research designs that integrate inductive analytics and abductive discovery to develop theory on these emerging concepts. Finally, guidelines that highlight the implications of trade-offs faced by platform providers while designing the platform are provided.

References

1. Karhade, P., Dong, J.Q.: Information technology investment and commercialized innovation performance: dynamic adjustment costs and curvilinear impacts. MIS Q. (2021, forthcoming)
2. Karhade, P., Dong, J.Q.: Innovation outcomes of digitally enabled collaborative problemistic search capability. MIS Q. (2021, forthcoming)
3. Dong, J.Q., Karhade, P., Rai, A., Xu, S.X.: How firms make information technology investment decisions: toward a behavioral agency theory. J. Manag. Inf. Syst. 38(1), 29–58 (2021)
4. Dong, J.Q., Karhade, P., Rai, A., Xu, S.X.: Information technology and innovation outputs: the missing link of search evolution. In: Academy of Management Proceedings 2015, vol. 1, p. 13847. Academy of Management, Briarcliff Manor (2015)

5. Dong, J.Q., He, J., Karhade, P.: The Penrose effect in resource investment for innovation: evidence from information technology and human capital. In: ECIS Completed Research, p. 80 (2013)
6. Andrade Rojas, M.G., Kathuria, A., Lee, H.-H.: Attaining operating performance through Pas De Trios of IT, competitive brokerage and innovation. In: Proceedings of the International Conference on Information Systems, Fort Worth (2015)
7. Ramakrishnan, T., Khuntia, J., Kathuria, A., Saldanha, T.J.V.: Business intelligence capabilities. In: Deokar, A.V., Gupta, A., Iyer, L.S., Jones, M.C. (eds.) Analytics and Data Science. AIS, pp. 15–27. Springer, Cham (2018). https://doi.org/10.1007/978-3-319-58097-5_3
8. Saldanha, T.J.V., Kathuria, A., Khuntia, J., Konsynski, B., Andrade Rojas, M.: Leveraging digitalization of services for performance: evidence from the credit union industry. In: Proceedings of the International Conference on Information Systems, Seoul (2017)
9. Tiwana, A., Konsynski, B., Bush, A.: Platform evolution: coevolution of platform architecture, governance, and environmental dynamics. Inf. Syst. Res. **21**(4), 675–687 (2010)
10. Chen, L., Xu, P., Liu, D.: Effect of crowd voting on participation in crowdsourcing contests. J. Manag. Inf. Syst. **37**(2), 510–535 (2020)
11. Karhade, P., Kathuria, A., Konsynski, B.: When choice matters: assortment and participation for performance on digital platforms. In: Proceedings of the 54th Hawaii International Conference on System Sciences, Maui, p. 1799 (2021)
12. Andrade Rojas, M., Saldanha, T., Khuntia, J., Kathuria, A., Boh, W.F.: Overcoming innovation deficiencies in Mexico: use of open innovation through IT and closed innovation through IT by small and medium enterprises. In: Proceedings of the 54th Hawaii International Conference on System Sciences, Maui, p. 617 (2021)
13. Kathuria, A., Saldanha, T., Khuntia, J., Andrade Rojas, M., Mithas, S., Hah, H.: Inferring supplier quality in the gig economy: the effectiveness of signals in freelance job markets. In: Proceedings of the 54th Hawaii International Conference on System Sciences, Maui, p. 6583 (2021)
14. Vitzthum, S., Kathuria, A., Konsynski, B.: Toys become tools: from virtual worlds to real commerce. Commun. Assoc. Inf. Syst. **29**, 379–394 (2011)
15. Kathuria, A., Karhade, P., Konsynski, B.R.: In the realm of hungry ghosts: multi-level theory for supplier participation on digital platforms. J. Manag. Inf. Syst. **37**(2), 396–430 (2020)
16. Karhade, P., Kathuria, A.: Missing impact of ratings on platform participation in India: a call for research in GREAT domains. Commun. Assoc. Inf. Syst. **47**(1), 19 (2020)
17. Dasgupta, A., Karhade, P., Kathuria, A., Konsynski, B.: Holding space for voices that do not speak: design reform of rating systems for platforms in GREAT economies. In: Proceedings of the 54th Hawaii International Conference on System Sciences, Maui, p. 2564 (2021)
18. Khuntia, J., Saldanha, T., Kathuria, A.: Dancing in the tigers' den: MNCs versus local firms leveraging IT-enabled strategic flexibility. In: Proceedings of the International Conference on Information Systems, Auckland (2014)
19. Kathuria, A., Khuntia, J., Karhade, P., Ning, X.: Don't ever take sides with anyone against the family: family ownership and information management. In: Proceedings of the Americas Conference on Information Systems, Cancun (2019)
20. Ning, X., Khuntia, J., Kathuria, A., Karhade, P.: Information technology investment, environmental hostility, and firm performance: the roles of family ownership in an emerging economy. In: Proceedings of the 53rd Hawaii International Conference on System Sciences, Maui (2020)
21. Ning, X., Khuntia, J., Kathuria, A., Karhade, P.: Ownership and management control effects on IT investments: a study of Indian family firms. In: Proceedings of the International Conference on Information Systems, Hyderabad (2020)
22. McIntyre, D.P., Srinivasan, A.: Networks, platforms, and strategy: emerging views and next steps. Strateg. Manag. J. **38**(1), 141–160 (2017)

23. Saldanha, T., Kathuria, A., Khuntia, J., Konsynski, B.: Ghosts in the machine: how marketing and human capital investments enhance customer growth when innovative services leverage self-service technologies. Inf. Syst. Res. (2021, forthcoming)
24. Karhade, P., Shaw, M.J., Subramanyam, R.: Patterns in information systems portfolio prioritization. MIS Q. **39**(2), 413–434 (2015)
25. Karhade, P.: IT portfolio management: an enterprise risk management-based perspective. In: AMCIS 2007 Proceedings, p. 405 (2007)
26. Karhade, P., Shaw, M.: Rejection and selection decisions in the IT portfolio composition process: an enterprise risk management based perspective. In: AMCIS 2007 Proceedings, p. 221 (2007)
27. Kathuria, A., Karhade, P.P.: You are not you when you are hungry: machine learning investigation of impact of ratings on ratee decision making. In: Xu, J.J., Zhu, B., Liu, X., Shaw, M.J., Zhang, H., Fan, M. (eds.) WEB 2018. LNBIP, vol. 357, pp. 151–161. Springer, Cham (2019). https://doi.org/10.1007/978-3-030-22784-5_15
28. Kathuria, A., Saldanha, T., Khuntia, J., Andrade Rojas, M.G., Hah, H.: Strategic intent, contract duration, and performance: evidence from micro-outsourcing. In: Proceedings of the International Conference on Information Systems, Fort Worth (2015)
29. Hukal, P., Henfridsson, O., Shaikh, M., Parker, G.: Platform signaling for generating platform content. MIS Q. **44**(3), 1177–1205 (2020)

Pins on the Map: Navigating the Ambiguous Landscape of Generativity in Digital Platform Ecosystems

Tobias Pauli[(✉)]

FAU Erlangen-Nürnberg, Fürther Str. 248, 90429 Nürnberg, Germany
tobias.pauli@fau.de

Abstract. Generativity is the main influencing mechanism for platform ecosystem evolution. As the literature on generativity grows, however, researchers have criticized that the concept itself remains rather fuzzy and ambiguous. Thus, the paper at hand aspires to make generativity more tangible. Based on a literature review, we uncover what is known about the nature, measurement, and management of generativity. Our results show that generativity is indeed still a somewhat elusive concept. While generativity is critical for the success of platform ecosystems, it also has negative effects. While there are valid approaches to measure generativity ex-post, leading indicators are still scarce. Lastly, while there are ways to manage generativity, the majority of the literature stresses its chaotic and serendipitous nature. By mapping the ambiguous landscape of generativity, we provide researchers and practitioners with a clearer understanding, further paving the way for generativity to become a valuable concept for understanding platform ecosystem evolution.

Keywords: Digital platform · Platform ecosystem · Generativity · Innovation

1   Introduction

As a major manifestation of e-business, digital platforms are centered on the premise of using the innovative capacities of a large ecosystem of actors outside the focal firm. Thus, they are often associated with generativity, defined as "a technology's overall capacity to produce unprompted change driven by large, varied, and uncoordinated audiences" [49, p. 1980]. Generativity has been identified as a major factor for platform ecosystem evolution, as complementors continuously develop new modules which in turn attract new customers [8].

As succinctly stated by Tiwana [41, p. 155] "the evolution of platform ecosystems is a journey [. . .]. In a journey, you need markers – pins on the map – [. . .] to decide whether you are indeed headed in the intended direction." Setting such

This research has been supported by the German Federal Ministry of Education and Research (FKZ 01 | S17045).

A. Garimella et al. (Eds.): WeB 2020, LNBIP 418, pp. 75–88, 2021.
https://doi.org/10.1007/978-3-030-79454-5_8

markers, however, requires a clear understanding of where one wants to go, one's current position, and potential routes to reach the desired destination.

To date, the literature on generativity has been characterized by a rather vague application of the concept. As Eck and Uebernickel [10, p. 2] state in their literature review on generativity, "there is no consensus on what the nature of generativity is and how it manifests itself". Although they subsequently considerably advance our understanding of generativity by specifying it as a result of system design and evolution, there are still many questions remaining. Thus, even though generativity is one of the main mechanisms that drives platform ecosystem evolution, its still rather fuzzy and ambiguous nature renders it a difficult basis for tracking the platform ecosystem journey.

The paper at hand aspires to provide support in setting pins on the map by addressing the following research questions: (1) How much generativity is desirable in digital platform ecosystems? (2) Which indicators can be used to operationalize or measure generativity along ecosystem evolution? (3) How can generativity be managed? To answer these research questions, we systematically review the growing body of literature on generativity.

As answering all these questions in-depth in a workshop paper is a daring endeavor, we do not claim to answer them conclusively. In fact, our results show that there may be no definitive answer for any of these questions. While a certain amount of generativity is desirable, too much generativity can have negative consequences. While there have been interesting and valid approaches to measure generativity ex-post, leading indicators for generativity are still scarce. Lastly, while there are ways to manage generativity, it seems to be mostly regarded as an inherent characteristic that, if actively influenced at all, should primarily be restricted instead of facilitated.

Instead, our intention and contribution are twofold: First, we want to show that although it is widely used, generativity is still an elusive concept in several dimensions. Second, in this way we also render it less elusive by mapping the landscape of generativity and thus providing researchers and practitioners alike with a clearer understanding.

The remainder of the paper is structured as follows. First, we provide some theoretical background on digital platform ecosystems and how their evolution is driven by generativity. Subsequently, we describe the methodological foundations of our literature review. In Sect. 4, we present our results on navigating the ambiguous landscape of generativity along three questions: Where do I want to go? Where am I? How do I get there? To conclude our paper, we discuss fruitful avenues for future research and how our results contribute to the literature on the generativity of digital platform ecosystems.

2   The Generative Evolution of Digital Platform Ecosystems

Platforms are one of the main trajectories of digital innovation [47]. While pure transaction platforms only act as a market intermediary, many platforms also perform the role of innovation platforms as "products, services, or technologies that [...] provide the foundation upon which outside firms [...] can provide their own complementary products, technologies, or services" [14, p. 418]. Digital platforms build on the premise that the functionality of digital products is somewhat decoupled from their physical form. As a consequence, their functionality can be extended after they have been physically "finished" [48]. To add functionalities, digital platforms usually rely on an ecosystem of third-party complementors. These complementors contribute to the platform by providing modular extensions that are compatible with the platform core. This enables platform owners to cover a heterogeneous market with varying customer needs while only offering a standardized core [44]. To describe the distributed innovation emerging in platform ecosystems, researchers refer to the notion of generativity.

Originating in psychology as "a need to nurture and guide younger people and contribute to the next generation" [29], the concept has spread across various disciplines from linguistics, over architecture, to organization science [3], each time with a slightly different meaning but keeping a creation and evolution aspect. In the mid-2000s, it was introduced to the information systems field primarily by Avital and Te'eni [3], and Zittrain [49]. Following Zittrain [49, p. 1980], whose definition of generativity is by far the most widely cited, generativity is "a technology's overall capacity to produce unprompted change driven by large, varied, and uncoordinated audiences". Thus, generativity is vital for a platform's evolution and survival, as it allows for the adaptation to unanticipated changes in the environment [12].

Sparked by Zittrain's seminal definition, researchers' interest in the topic has flourished in the past decade. A large part of the discourse has taken place in the information systems literature and more specifically the literature on digital platform ecosystems. Despite or precisely because of its popularity, generativity remains a rather ambiguous concept, used by many researchers as "a nice shorthand label for a crucial and complicated thought" [36, p. 2758].

As a result, other researchers have already tried to clear the mist. Noting the increasing proliferation of generativity in information systems research, Eck et al. [9] analyze the different meanings assigned to the term. In a subsequent article, criticizing the fuzziness of the concept, Eck and Uebernickel [10] set out to provide a more clear-cut definition of generativity. Arguing that the ambiguity of the concept in information systems research is inter alia caused by the missing clarity of Zittrain's [49] definition, they scrutinize this definition to clarify it. Subsequently, they derive two perspectives on generativity: generativity as a consequence of a system's design, and generativity as a consequence of a system's evolution.

Despite these valuable efforts, generativity is still "conceived as a seemingly chaotic and anarchic environment" [20, p. 983]. Knowing that generativity can both be understood from a rather static design perspective and a dynamic evolutionary perspective still leaves some open questions: How much generativity is desirable? Is generativity always good? How can we measure generativity? How can we manage generativity? In this article, we will try to provide tentative answers to these questions by reviewing extant literature on the generativity of digital platform ecosystems.

3   Method

To answer our research questions, we conducted a systematic literature review. According to Templier and Paré [39] our study can be characterized as a narrative review with the objective of summarizing the literature on the generativity of digital platform ecosystems. Nevertheless, as many literature reviews cannot reasonably be assigned to a single ideal type [26], it also entails elements of a descriptive review [34]. Therefore, while purely narrative reviews often rely on a subjective and non-systematic literature selection process, we conducted a systematic literature search as proposed by Webster and Watson [45].

We started our literature review by scanning the AIS Senior Scholar's Basket of Eight for papers with "generativity" in their title or abstract. This yielded 231[1] papers as a result, with 12 relevant papers remaining after a screening of first title and abstract, and later the full text.

Because of the low number of results and the generativity concept's origin outside the information systems discipline, we subsequently searched Scopus, again for papers with "generativity" in their title or abstract. This search resulted in an additional 1181 articles.

After screening the title and abstract, 15 papers remained from the basket and 71 papers from Scopus. At this point, we removed papers that discussed generativity in a different meaning (such as in developmental psychology) or in a setting with no connection to digital platforms. Consequently, the interdisciplinary nature of the concept led to the dismissal of a large number of articles at this stage. However, while we focused on generativity in digital platform ecosystems, we kept an open mind regarding papers addressing the generativity of digital technologies and infrastructures in a more general sense.

In the next step, we screened the full text of the remaining 86 papers to assess their relevance for our research questions. In this step, we removed 21 papers from our dataset, mostly because of an only tangential consideration of generativity. Based on a subsequent check for duplicates between our Basket and Scopus sets, we removed 3 papers. In the last step, a backward search identified 6 additional relevant papers, resulting in a final set of 68 papers for our analysis.

We did not conduct a forward search because of two reasons. First, we already followed a rather broad search strategy by looking for papers mentioning "generativity" in their title and abstract in the entire Scopus database. Second, the seminal papers by Zittrain [49,50] have already been cited over 2 500 times, rendering a forward search rather complex and unfeasible. As our aim is to provide a representative and approximately comprehensive overview of the literature, this approach seemed appropriate.

---

[1] This number is rather high because the journal search engines sometimes used truncation automatically (e.g., leading to inclusion of "generate" or "generation") or only supported full text search.

We coded the final set of papers using the qualitative data analysis software MAXQDA. This allowed us to identify common themes across papers and define categories. While we primarily coded in a deductive manner based on our research questions, we also created new categories inductively to allow for uncovering (implicit) assumptions in the literature [26].

4 Mapping the Ambiguous Landscape of Generativity

4.1 Towards Generativity: Where Do I Want to Go?

Naturally, before setting out on a journey, one should determine the destination. In terms of generativity, even though it is characterized by "unanticipated" change, it might be worthwhile to determine the desired amount of generativity in the platform ecosystem. As discussed earlier, generativity is one of the main drivers of platform evolution. As such, it seems like generativity is a desirable or even necessary characteristic of digital platform ecosystems. However, the literature also discusses downsides of generativity as well as factors that need to be balanced with generativity.

Generally, generativity is viewed as something positive and even the main factor for the success of digital platforms [30]. Avital and Te'eni [3, p. 347], for example, explicitly refer to it as "a productive capacity that focuses on creating something that is beneficial and desirable". As an obvious positive effect, generativity increases innovation and extends the functionality of platforms [10,50]. This, in turn, increases the overall success of the platform ecosystem by triggering positive system reputation and network effects [8].

While generativity is thus imperative for successful digital platform ecosystems, more generativity is not necessarily better. Indeed, generativity comes with different pitfalls, as evident from many of the papers in our literature review. In their study of video game platforms, Cennamo and Santaló [8], for example, find evidence for a negative free-riding effect. In the early stages of platform ecosystem evolution, generativity ensures a steady flow of new games to satisfy diverse customer preferences. However, as the ecosystem matures and competition with other platforms increases, a tension arises between a positive reputation spillover effect and a negative free-rider effect. In this setting, a high number of high-quality contributions that increases overall platform reputation leads to reduced incentives for individuals to invest more resources into the development of complements, as they can "get away" with lower quality as well.

The resulting variance in complements is a negative effect of generativity frequently mentioned in literature. Nielsen and Hanseth [31], for example, state that the development of contributions by heterogeneous audiences can lead to a fragmented landscape of offerings. This fragmentation might result in customer insecurity and lower satisfaction because of low-quality complements [8]. In other cases, it can lead to modules that are not (fully) compatible with the platform core [30].

Based on these negative implications of generativity, researchers mention several tensions between generativity and other factors. A classic tension discussed in literature on platform ecosystems is the trade-off between autonomy and control [44]. This tension is also echoed in generativity literature [12]. As generativity is dependent on "uncoordinated audiences", complementor autonomy is necessarily a prerequisite for generativity. However, too little control can lead to the aforementioned negative results such as low-quality complements and fragmentation of the ecosystem [47].

This is closely related to balancing generativity and usability. While early adopters accept and even embrace complexity, mainstream users want products with a more confined set of functions that are easy to use. Therefore, usually, technologies follow a trajectory from complex, feature-driven architectures to simpler, more usability-driven designs [33]. To some extent, this clashes with the generativity of digital platforms. Having an ecosystem of heterogeneous actors developing complementary innovations will almost inevitably lead to a plethora of features. As Nielsen and Hanseth [31] discuss along the case of the iPhone, platform owners need to find ways to ensure high levels of generativity and usability at the same time.

A third balancing factor for generativity is standardization [16]. In contrast to the aforementioned ones, however, this trade-off is not focused on limiting potential negative effects of too much or uncontrolled generativity. Instead, it relates to the balancing act of standardizing IT infrastructure to the largest extent possible, while at the same time keeping generativity high. Standardization is desirable because it allows for the reuse of components, enabling economies of scale [40]. Standardization is also necessary for generativity, as it facilitates accessibility and adaptability as important prerequisites for generativity [50]. On the other hand, too much standardization can also stifle generativity [16,44]. Thus, the challenge in digital platform ecosystems is to balance standardization and generativity in such a way that one can reap the benefits of both.

In the end, it is difficult to determine a universal answer to the question of the desired amount of generativity. As often, the sweet spot seems to be somewhere in the middle. Generativity is without doubt necessary for a platform ecosystem to thrive. However, too much generativity can lead to fragmented ecosystems with patchy complement quality and customer insecurity.

4.2   Measuring Generativity: Where Am I?

As mentioned earlier, for the most part, "generativity is conceived as a seemingly chaotic and anarchic environment" [20, p. 983]. At the same time, it is something that needs to be delicately balanced with other factors. However, doing so requires indicators concerning the level of generativity in the platform ecosystem. Therefore, we scanned the identified literature for lagging and also potential leading indicators of generativity that could help assess generativity and subsequently guide the evolution of digital platform ecosystems.

Lagging indicators look backwards in time and serve to tell whether a platform ecosystem has thus far been generative. Consequently, they represent the results of generativity. In line with the criticized ambiguity, the results of generativity are often referred to on a rather high level. Zittrain's [49] original definition refers to "unprompted change". In the information systems literature on digital platform ecosystems, this change has been equated with innovation [30, 46]. On a lower level, this innovation is often specified as new services [31, 43] or applications [23, 43].

Eck et al. [9, p. 13] criticize this equation of generativity and innovation, stating that "unanticipated outcomes do not have to be innovations, there might be other worthwhile ends to be considered". While other manifestations of generativity are mentioned in the literature, they also remain rather vague. Examples include "new outputs, structures or behaviors" [27, p. 54] or "new supplementary modules, organizational structures, and work practices" [22, p. 2010]. However, the innovation aspect is present in these examples as well, as all authors mention that the created "things" are usually new.

Most of these lagging indicators are rather vague in nature. Thus, our results are in line with Le Masson et al. [25, p. 7] who found that generativity "is usually hardly quantified". However, there are also a few papers that attempt to operationalize the measurement of generativity in empirical studies.

Andersen and Bogusz [2] study the evolution of a blockchain-based infrastructure over several years. To analyze the generative evolution of the blockchain infrastructure, they rely on forking events, that is, splitting off source code to pursue an independent line of development, as an operationalization. Interestingly, Fürstenau et al. [13] follow a similar approach. Their object of interest is the digital web-shop platform of Otto, a German e-commerce company. To study the generativity-driven evolution of the platform, they also rely on forking in the platform's GitHub repository. Cennamo and Santaló [8] apply a more straightforward and intuitive approach in their study of generativity-related tensions in platform ecosystems. Their study relies on longitudinal data from the U.S. video game industry. To determine the degree of generativity, they use the number and diversity of games launched in a certain month for a certain platform. This is in line with Nikou et al. [32] who suggest the variety of complements as an appropriate indicator.

Hein et al. [18] again employ two different criteria to measure generativity. To assess the amount of generativity, they use complementors' autonomy and the degree of knowledge sharing as indicators. In turn, to operationalize autonomy they analyze the number of complementors and whether their relationship with the platform owner is characterized by tight or loose coupling. For the assessment of knowledge sharing they rely on the number of active GitHub repositories. Um et al. [42] study the evolution of the WordPress platform. In their approach inspired by network biology, they indicate the number of complementary plug-ins as a measure for generativity.

What becomes obvious from these examples is that generativity, of course, cannot be measured directly. Instead, researchers employ different proxies. While some of those, such as the variety of complements, might be relatively easy to determine, others, for example knowledge sharing, might themselves again require proxies for measurement. Additionally, all presented studies and indicators focus on an ex-post determination of generativity. With the exception of the measures used by Hein et al. [18], none of the criteria can be used as leading indicators for generativity. Overall, it seems difficult to exactly determine a system's generativity. Interestingly, the generativity of some kinds of digital platforms might be easier to determine as there are digital traces for many actions, such as in the case of repositories like GitHub.

4.3   Managing Generativity: How Do I Get There?

Sticking to the navigation analogy, after having found out where one wants to go and having defined one's current position, the last step is to figure out how to reach the desired destination. With regard to generativity, this refers to influencing the amount of generativity in a given platform ecosystem.

The majority of the literature treats generativity as an inherent capability of digital platform ecosystems, making achieving generativity rather easy. This serendipitous nature of generativity is already noticeable in Zittrain's [49, p. 1980] seminal definition of generativity as "a technology's overall capacity to produce unprompted change driven by large, varied, and uncoordinated audiences". It suggests that generativity is a characteristic of a certain system or technology. A majority of the literature building on this definition thus adopts this perspective, leading to the overall impression that once certain conditions are fulfilled, generativity "evolves endogenously, without prior planning or central control" [46, p. 3].

Taking a more detailed look, there are several characteristics that make a technology or phenomenon generative. Zittrain [50] mentions capacity for leverage, adaptability, ease of mastery, and accessibility. With regard to digital technologies, there are additional characteristics that facilitate generativity. These include modularity [43], openness [21, 37], standardization [16] and incompleteness [38]. All of these characteristics reflect the layered modular architecture of digital innovation as described by Yoo et al. [48]. Not surprisingly, many of these characteristics can be found in digital platforms, illuminating why generativity is for the most part implicitly regarded as an inherent capability.

Consequently, based on this notion of generativity as something that spreads somewhat automatically, the main challenge does not seem to be to foster generativity, but to restrict it. This is in line with the large part of literature focusing on generativity-related trade-offs discussed earlier. To restrict generativity, platform owners can employ different measures. By exerting control over interfaces and access to the ecosystem, they can determine who can interact with the platform in which way [15, 30]. Additionally, platform owners can control type and quality of complements ex-post by checking them against a standard policy [8].

These approaches to influence generativity interestingly rely primarily on governing actors' interaction with the platform. This points toward an aspect of generativity that goes beyond a platform's or technology's generative properties. While on the one hand a certain generative potential is ascribed to technologies and systems based on their design, on the other hand, generativity (especially in digital platforms) is always closely linked to evolutionary dynamics, i.e. how generative a technology really is will only show after the ecosystem has interacted with it for a certain amount of time [1,10,38].

This interaction of users with a generative technology or platform as the key factor for realization of its generative potential is a recurring theme in literature [1,9,10,50]. Thus, importantly, generativity is a socio-technical phenomenon and needs to be understood and analyzed accordingly [30]. As a consequence, besides technical characteristics of the platform, there are also features of the ecosystem such as the frequently mentioned heterogeneity of actors [5,9,20,24,30,47] that have a positive influence on generativity.

In conclusion, our analysis of the literature indicates that while the two perspectives of generativity as a consequence of system design, and as a consequence of system evolution proposed by Eck and Uebernickel [10] are reflected in the approaches to manage generativity, they are employed in different ways. While the facilitation of generativity primarily focuses on the creation of generative characteristics at the point of system design, the restriction of generativity is centered around controlling platform ecosystem evolution. Broadly speaking, there seems to be an implicit assumption that once a system is designed "generatively", the main task is to restrict generativity and not foster it.

From a different perspective, according to Blaschke and Brosius [6, p. 2] "generativity can only be stimulated (not directly managed) by control mechanisms that appropriately bound participant behavior without excessively constraining a desired level of generativity". While this might initially sound somewhat contradicting, it makes sense in light of the abovementioned insights from literature. "Control" in terms of generativity does not necessarily mean restricting the amount of generativity in a platform ecosystem. Similarly, "stimulate" does not necessarily refer to increasing the amount of generativity. Instead, both stimulation and control refer to channeling a platform ecosystem's generativity in the desired direction. The result is a "continuous process of developers as protagonists seeking to engage in generative acts [...] and an opposing platform owner as antagonist [...] accepting or rejecting generative attempts" [11, p. 272].

5 Discussion

Generativity is a concept frequently used in platform ecosystems research. This is not surprising, given the domains and cases most frequently studied. Many studies focus on mobile platforms [4,15] or video game platforms [7,8]. These platforms come relatively close to the prerequisites for generativity proposed by Zittrain [50] such as adaptability, ease of mastery, and accessibility [9]. This might be one of the main reasons for the implicit assumption that generativity is an inherent characteristic of digital platform ecosystems. However, while this might be true for many or even most of the digital platforms studied to date, it may not be valid as a general rule.

As the "platformization" affects more and more branches of the economy [35], platforms emerge that do not unanimously fulfill these criteria. A phenomenon that is increasingly attracting the attention of researchers in information systems, for example, are Industrial Internet of Things (IIoT) platforms [17,19]. These platforms collect data from a heterogeneous set of industrial assets and machines and provide it to third parties for the development and sales of industrial applications. Thus, they are a major trajectory of industrial firms' increasing move towards e-business [28]. Such technologically more complex platforms may not be characterized by ease of mastery. Similarly, the ecosystems around them will not resemble "large, varied, and uncoordinated" [49, p. 1980] audiences, but may be more closed business-to-business networks with distinct governance. To provide meaningful analyses of the evolution of such platform ecosystems, we need to move away from regarding every digital platform as being inherently generative.

In line with this change of perspective, we need to increasingly identify means to deliberately foster generativity. This needs to go beyond designing static properties of systems to ensuring ecosystem interaction along the lifecycle. The literature currently focuses on passive characteristics and not active measures. This means, to some extent, setting the stage for generativity primarily in the beginning of the life cycle and then letting it play out. This notion of the serendipitous nature of generativity is somewhat problematic, as "we cannot simply assume that systems continue to evolve generatively on the sole basis of their generative history" [10, p. 4].

Adopting a more proactive perspective on generativity also includes defining more specific measures to assess the generativity of digital platform ecosystems. As our results show, generativity is often equated with innovation. As a consequence, a platform ecosystem is regarded as generative if it can produce a high number or variety of complements. However, this clashes to some extent with the ambiguous nature of generativity as being desired on the one hand, and detrimental at some point. As Cennamo and Santaló [8, p. 618] put it, "not all complements are created equal". Some complements might be more valuable for the platform ecosystem than others that might even have a negative impact. Researchers should therefore aim for more clearly specified indicators of generativity. This will not only allow for a more precise application of the concept, but also aid in the abovementioned design of mechanisms to facilitate generativity. Otherwise, as Eck and Uebernickel [10, p. 2] put it, "there is no point trying to design 'for generativity' or 'towards generativity' because we do not know which design objectives to aim for".

6   Conclusion

In this paper, we attempted to map the ambiguous landscape of generativity in digital platform ecosystems along three questions: (1) How much generativity is desirable in digital platform ecosystems? (2) Which indicators can be used to operationalize or measure generativity along ecosystem evolution? (3) How can generativity be managed? Our analysis shows that, despite the valuable efforts by Eck and Uebernickel [10], and Eck et al. [9], the literature on generativity still seems to suffer from the concept's character as "a nice shorthand label for a crucial and complicated thought" [36, p. 2758]. While generativity is critical for the success of platform ecosystems, it also has negative effects. While there are valid approaches to measure generativity ex-post, leading indicators are still scarce. Lastly, while there are ways to manage generativity, its seemingly chaotic and serendipitous nature leads to a focus on restriction rather than facilitation.

However, the aim of this paper is not necessarily to criticize this ambiguity, as it is to some extent part of the nature of generativity itself. "Unprompted change driven by large, varied, and uncoordinated audiences" [49, p. 1980] can perhaps by definition not be planned, measured and managed precisely. Still, while the generativity-driven evolutionary journey of different platform ecosystems will be unique, it still needs to be restricted and facilitated, and thus channeled in the right direction [41]. This requires a clear understanding of the desired level of generativity, the current level of generativity, and appropriate mechanisms to reconcile the both. In other words, it requires pins on the map that guide the platform evolution. The paper at hand provides help in setting such pins as it explores what we know about the means to measure and manage generativity.

Thus, by mapping the ambiguous landscape of generativity, our study contributes to the literature on the generativity of digital platform ecosystems by providing a clearer understanding of the nature of generativity. While this does not resolve the ambiguity inherent to the concept, it allows for a more precise handling by both researchers and practitioners. When studying generativity in different empirical contexts, researchers can build on our insights to more clearly specify their underlying assumptions and preconceptions regarding the concept. Practitioners, on the other hand, can use this study as a guideline regarding the assessment and management of generativity as their platforms evolve. Especially as domains are seized by platformization that may not be inherently generative, such as the IIoT, it will be vital to actively manage generativity.

Of course, as a limitation, this workshop paper can only provide tentative answers to the three research questions. Still, it can serve as a starting point for further exploration and clarification. This clarification is necessary in order for generativity to remain a valuable concept for research on digital platform ecosystems.

References

1. Bygstad, B.: Generative innovation: a comparison of lightweight and heavyweight IT. J. Inf. Technol. **32**(2), 180–193 (2017)
2. Andersen, J.V., Bogusz, C.I.: Self-organizing in blockchain infrastructures: generativity through shifting objectives and forking. J. Assoc. Inf. Syst. **20**(9), 1242–1273 (2019)
3. Avital, M., Te'eni, D.: From generative fit to generative capacity: exploring an emerging dimension of information systems design and task performance. Inf. Syst. J. **19**(4), 345–367 (2009)
4. Basole, R.C., Karla, J.: On the evolution of mobile platform ecosystem structure and strategy. Bus. Inf. Syst. Engi. **3**(5), 313–322 (2011). https://doi.org/10.1007/s12599-011-0174-4

5. Bergvall-Kåreborn, B., Howcroft, D.: Persistent problems and practices in information systems development: a study of mobile applications development and distribution. Inf. Syst. J. **24**(5), 425–444 (2014)
6. Blaschke, M.R., Brosius, M.: Digital platforms: balancing control and generativity. In: Proceedings of the 39th International Conference on Information Systems, San Francisco, USA, pp. 1–9 (2018)
7. Cennamo, C., Ozalp, H., Kretschmer, T.: Platform architecture and quality trade-offs of multihoming complements. Inf. Syst. Res. **29**(2), 461–478 (2018)
8. Cennamo, C., Santaló, J.: Generativity tension and value creation in platform ecosystems. Organ. Sci. **30**(3), 617–641 (2019)
9. Eck, A., Uebernickel, F., Brenner, W.: The generative capacity of digital artifacts: a mapping of the field. In: Proceedings of the 19th Pacific Asia Conference on Information Systems, Singapore, pp. 1–20 (2015)
10. Eck, A., Uebernickel, F.: Untangling generativity: two perspectives on unanticipated change produced by diverse actors. In: Proceedings of the 24th European Conference on Information Systems, Istanbul, Turkey, pp. 1–19 (2016)
11. Elaluf-Calderwood, S.M., Eaton, B.D., Sørensen, C., Yoo, Y.: Control as a strategy for the development of generativity in business models for mobile platforms. In: 3rd International Workshop on Business Models for Mobile Platforms, Berlin, Germany, pp. 271–276 (2011)
12. Foerderer, J., Kude, T., Schuetz, S.W., Heinzl, A.: Control versus generativity: a complex adaptive systems perspective on service platforms. In: Proceedings of the 35th International Conference on Information Systems, Auckland, New Zealand, pp. 1–13 (2014)
13. Fürstenau, D., et al.: Growth, complexity, and generativity of digital platforms: the case of Otto.de. In: Proceedings of the 40th International Conference on Information Systems, Munich, Germany, pp. 1–16 (2019)
14. Gawer, A., Cusumano, M.A.: Industry platforms and ecosystem innovation. J. Prod. Innov. Manag. **31**(3), 417–433 (2014)
15. Ghazawneh, A., Henfridsson, O.: Balancing platform control and external contribution in third-party development: the boundary resources model. Inf. Syst. J. **23**(2), 173–192 (2013)
16. Grisot, M., Vassilakopoulou, P.: Infrastructures in healthcare: the interplay between generativity and standardization. Int. J. Med. Inform. **82**(5), e170–e179 (2013)
17. Hanelt, A., Nischak, F., Markus, N., Hodapp, D., Schneider, S.: Building platform ecosystems for IoT - exploring the impact on industrial-age firms. In: Proceedings of the 28th European Conference on Information Systems, pp. 1–17 (2020)
18. Hein, A., Setzke, D.S., Hermes, S., Weking, J.: The influence of digital affordances and generativity on digital platform leadership. In: Proceedings of the 40th International Conference on Information Systems, Munich, Germany, pp. 1–9 (2019)
19. Hodapp, D., Hawlitschek, F., Kramer, D.: Value co-creation in nascent platform ecosystems: a delphi study in the context of the Internet of Things. In: Proceedings of the 40th International Conference on Information Systems, Munich, Germany (2019)
20. Jarvenpaa, S.L., Standaert, W.: Digital probes as opening possibilities of generativity. J. Assoc. Inf. Syst. **19**(10), 982–1000 (2018)
21. Knol, A., Klievink, B., Tan, Y.H.: Data sharing issues and potential solutions for adoption of information infrastructures: evidence from a data pipeline project in the global supply chain over sea. In: Proceedings of the 27th BLED eConference, Bled, Slovenia, pp. 1–12 (2014)

22. Kretzer, M., Maedche, A.: Generativity of business intelligence platforms: a research agenda guided by lessons from shadow IT. In: Proceedings of the Multi-konferenz Wirtschaftsinformatik, Paderborn, Germany, pp. 207–220 (2014)
23. Lakemond, N., Holmberg, G.: Digital innovation in complex systems-managing critical applications and generativity. In: 31st Congress of the International Council of the Aeronautical Sciences, Belo Horizonte, Brazil, pp. 1–9 (2018)
24. Lane, D.A.: Complexity and innovation dynamics. In: Antonelli, C. (ed.) Handbook on the Economic Complexity of Technological Change, pp. 63–80. Edward Elgar, Cheltenham (2011)
25. Le Masson, P., Hatchuel, A., Kokshagina, O., Weil, B.: Generic technique and the dynamics of technologies: using matroid and design theory to design techniques with systemic impact. In: Proceedings of the 20th International Conference on Engineering Design, Milan, Italy, pp. 55–64 (2015)
26. Leidner, D.E.: Review and theory symbiosis: an introspective retrospective. J. Assoc. Inf. Syst. **19**(6), 552–567 (2018)
27. Lyytinen, K., Yoo, Y., Boland, R.J.: Digital product innovation within four classes of innovation networks. Inf. Syst. J. **26**(1), 47–75 (2016)
28. Martín-Peña, M., Díaz-Garrido, E., Sánchez-López, J.: The digitalization and servi-tization of manufacturing: a review on digital business models. Strateg. Chang. **27**(2), 91–99 (2018)
29. Generativity. Merriam-Webster. https://www.merriam-webster.com/medical/generativity. Accessed 6 Oct 2020
30. Msiska, B., Nielsen, P.: Innovation in the fringes of software ecosystems: the role of socio-technical generativity. Inf. Technol. Dev. **24**(2), 398–421 (2018)
31. Nielsen, P., Hanseth, O.: Towards a design theory of usability and generativity. In: Proceedings of the 18th European Conference on Information Systems, Pretoria, South Africa, pp. 1–13 (2010)
32. Nikou, S., Bouwman, H., Reuver, M.: A consumer perspective on mobile service platforms: a conjoint analysis approach. Commun. Assoc. Inf. Syst. **34**(1), 1409–1424 (2014)
33. Norman, D.A.: The Invisible Computer. MIT Press, Cambridge (1999)
34. Paré, G., Trudel, M.C., Jaana, M., Kitsiou, S.: Synthesizing information systems knowledge: a typology of literature reviews. Inf. Manag. **52**(2), 183–199 (2015)
35. Parker, G., Van Alstyne, M., Jiang, X.: Platform ecosystems: how developers invert the firm. MIS Q. **41**(1), 255–266 (2017)
36. Post, D.G.: The theory of generativity. Fordham Law Rev. **78**(6), 2755–2766 (2010)
37. Remneland-Wikhamn, B., Ljungberg, J.A.N., Bergquist, M., Kuschel, J.: Open innovation, generativity and the supplier as peer: the case of iphone and android. Int. J. Innov. Manag. **15**(1), 205–230 (2011)
38. da Rocha, F.N., Pollock, N.: Innovating in digital platforms - an integrative app-roach. In: Proceedings of the 21st International Conference on Enterprise Informa-tion Systems, Edinburgh, UK, pp. 505–515 (2019)
39. Templier, M., Paré, G.: A framework for guiding and evaluating literature reviews. Commun. Assoc. Inf. Syst. **37**(1), 112–137 (2015)
40. Thomas, L.D., Autio, E., Gann, D.M.: Architectural leverage: putting platforms in context. Acad. Manag. Perspect. **28**(2), 198–219 (2014)
41. Tiwana, A.: Platform Ecosystems: Aligning Architecture, Governance, and Strat-egy. Morgan Kaufmann, Amsterdam (2014)
42. Um, S., Yoo, Y., Wattal, S.: The evolution of digital ecosystems: a case of Word-Press from 2004 to 2014. In: Proceedings of the 36th International Conference on Information Systems, Fort Worth, USA, pp. 1–16 (2015)

43. Vassilakoupoulou, P., Grisot, M.: Technology innovation in the face of uncertainty: the case of 'my health record'. In: Proceedings of the 20th European Conference on Information Systems, Barcelona, Spain, pp. 1–12 (2012)
44. Wareham, J., Fox, P.B., Giner, J.L.C.: Technology ecosystem governance. Organ. Sci. **25**(4), 1195–1215 (2014)
45. Webster, J., Watson, R.T.: Analyzing the past to prepare for the future: writing a literature review. MIS Q. **26**(2), xiii–xxiii (2002)
46. Woodard, C.J., Clemons, E.K.: Modeling the evolution of generativity and the emergence of digital ecosystems. In: Proceedings of the 35th International Conference on Information Systems, Auckland, New Zealand, pp. 1–13 (2014)
47. Yoo, Y., Boland, R.J., Lyytinen, K., Majchrzak, A.: Organizing for innovation in the digitized world. Organ. Sci. **23**(5), 1398–1408 (2012)
48. Yoo, Y., Henfridsson, O., Lyytinen, K.: The new organizing logic of digital innovation: an agenda for information systems research. Inf. Syst. Res. **21**(4), 724–735 (2010)
49. Zittrain, J.: The generative internet. Harv. Law Rev. **119**(7), 1974–2040 (2006)
50. Zittrain, J.: Saving the internet. Harv. Bus. Rev. **85**(6), 49–59 (2007)

Managing Human Factors in e-Business

Digital Inclusion of Farmers and Rural Hinterland: The Case of Digital India

Amandeep Dhaliwal[✉]

FMS, Manav Rachna International Institute of Research and Studies, Faridabad, Haryana, India
amandeep.fms@mriu.edu.in

Abstract. Success in the increasingly digitized social and economic realms requires a comprehensive approach to fostering inclusion. India with world's largest digitally excluded population, undertook a major technology-based initiative - Digital India, to ensure digital inclusion of all. This qualitative study analyzes the various digital initiatives that are focused on rural sectors especially the farmers and agriculturists from the perspective of the Digital inclusion framework. It also investigates the current implementation status of these e-services and applications and the challenges involved along with some suggestive solutions. The results reflect that these initiatives are achieving digital inclusion to some extent but it still needs much more impetus and progress. This unique research presents the holistic view of these rural initiatives which can prove to be useful for other researchers and the policymakers in understanding and chalking out an action plan for enhancing rural digital inclusion through e-services and mobile applications globally.

Keywords: Digital inclusion · Digital India · Digital divide · Rural development · Digital transformation

1 Introduction

The ubiquity of the internet has fostered a new set of opportunities and challenges for individuals and communities. Digital Technology, no doubt has opened pathways to a new, highly interconnected world but on the other hand, it has also lead to the growth of a new domain of Digital divide and digital exclusion wherein some communities and populations have stayed isolated and aloof from this digital access, leading to even farther technological distance between the digitally included and digitally excluded categories and hence the inequitable distribution of opportunities between these two (India Exclusion Report 2017).

India a nation of 1.33 billion people is a prime example of such a digital divide. The World Development Report 2018 has revealed that almost 1.063 billion Indians were offline (World Development Report 2018). While another McKinsey report (Kaka et al. 2020) on digitized nations 2019 stated that though India had 560 million internet subscribers in September 2018, second only to China. India is the second-fastest digitizing

© Springer Nature Switzerland AG 2021
A. Garimella et al. (Eds.): WeB 2020, LNBIP 418, pp. 91–110, 2021.
https://doi.org/10.1007/978-3-030-79454-5_9

country but the overall score on the Adoption index is low 32 on the scale of 100 hence it still has a lot of growth potential.

Digital exclusion is astoundingly present especially in the rural areas and the villages of India. Poverty is the main reason for it. As per India Exclusion Report 2016, close to 1 billion people belonging to the lower-income group and belonging to rural areas do not have internet access in India nor the ability for Internet connectivity to access digital information. Agriculture and the farmers form the backbone of the Indian economy. Hence bringing them into the digital mainstream and exposing them to new technologies and information was vitally important. Realizing the negative consequences of the digital divide and exclusion, many initiatives based on e-services, web portals, and mobile applications have been taken and are being undertaken by the Government of India to ensure digital inclusion.

Digital India Program launched by the Indian government in 2015, focusing on three main areas of access to digital infrastructure, high-speed internet, digital identity, mobile phone & bank account services, cybersecurity, access to e-governance services and digital literacy and digital empowerment of all. This paper analyzes the initiatives for Digital inclusion in relation to the e-services based schemes and sub-programs and technology/mobile apps that have been launched under Digital India especially catering to agriculture and farmers to bring them into the digital mainstream. It further investigates the implementation and goal achievement of these initiatives and the hurdles which are there. Lastly, it suggests some solutions which can make this program a success.

2   Literature Review

2.1   Digital Inclusion

Digital inclusion as a coined term finds its existence first in academic literature around 2002–2003 (Warschuaer 2004; Correa 2008). It has its origins from the earlier literature on the 'digital divide'. Digital Divide as a concept was presented in the 1990s in the US where it was presented as "exclusion from information" due to inaccessibility of the internet and other ICT's (Campos-Castillo 2015; Walton et al. 2013). The digital divide was defined as the gap between the "haves" and "have-nots" (van Dijk 2006). The earlier inclusion policies, therefore, centered on ensuring access to the internet for everyone (Rose et al. 2014).

Bradbrook and Fisher (2004) were the first ones to define digital inclusion in terms of 5 'C's: connectivity (access), capability (skill), content, confidence (self-efficacy), and continuity. As the access to the internet and ICT increased, the focus of researchers moved on to how people use or do not use ICTs (Livingstone and Helsper 2007; Van Deursen et al. 2015). Especially after the "bubble burst" or the "dot com" crash, there was an expansion in the concept of digital inclusion as researchers began linking it with broader issues of social participation and inclusion, the availability of opportunities, the socio-economic disadvantages of excluded population, etc. (Warschuaer 2004; Selwyn and Facer 2007; Pearce and Rice 2013).

Further elaborating on the evolution of digital inclusion as a concept, the present-day researchers do not believe that it is limited to internet penetration. It goes beyond the access and involves a multidimensional process (Robinson et al. 2015). This complete digital inclusion process involves other dimensions such as type and quality of access, digital skills, and different types of uses of the internet (Correa and Pavez 2016; Hargittai and Hinnant 2008; Goggin et al. 2018).

At present Digital Inclusion is bearing increasingly important consequences that affect society such as informational, social, and economical integration of people, access to opportunities, social participation, community, and civic engagement. It is now considered fundamental human rights. Digital inclusion now is often projected as an alternative solution to gaps in contemporary society: poverty, social inequality, educational needs, social injustice, unemployment, violence, and crime, among others (Bonilla and Pretto 2011; Correa et al. 2020). Digital Inclusion Index (ADII), which defines digital inclusion as the capacity of people to access, afford, and use online technologies effectively.

Digital inclusion (van Dijk 2006; Brotcorne 2016; Ekbia 2016) as a concept has three broad aspects to it that help in creating inclusive communities.

- Access: Availability, affordability, and public access.
- Adoption: digital literacy, and consumer safety.
- Application: Across various sectors - education, health care, public safety, and emergency services, civic engagement, and e-governance.

Based on these aspects the digital inclusion has been extensively studied amongst the various stakeholder groups such as digital inclusion amongst several marginalized groups including seniors (Sum et al. 2008), Children (Notley 2009), Indigenous Australians (Letch and Carroll 2008), isolated communities (Correa et al. 2017), gender (Gray et al. 2017), young people with a disability (Newman et al. 2017), lower-income families (Katz 2017), refugees (Alam et al. 2015) and rural and remote residents (Walton et al. 2013).

The digital Inclusion of rural communities is of particular importance. Townsend et al. (2013) in their study presented the multifaceted benefits of the 'connected' rural communities, including the attraction of workers and their families to rural areas. Similarly, Roberts et al. (2017) explored the topic of 'Harnessing digital technologies and crossing divides' focusing on the challenges, uses, and benefits for the user and non-user of the internet in rural areas. They establish a clear link between digital inclusion and rural resilience, proposing that "key resilience terms are especially helpful for thinking about how and why communities benefit or become disadvantaged in the ways they do".

Digital exclusion is no longer a 'minor' issue rather it has a large disadvantageous effect on the population which is not included (Leung 2014). Ewing et al. (2018) exclaimed that "Those who are not connected now, and in the future, maybe fewer, but they will be missing out on far more – in education, health, e-government, commerce, communication, and entertainment – than the nonusers of previous decades".

Though the term "digital divide" is still widely used but digital inclusion is a more holistic concept, as it recognizes the fact that we can have a more inclusive society only when all individuals can utilize the benefits of digital technologies and use them for democratic participation and social inclusion afforded by connectivity (Willis and Tranter 2006; Walton et al. 2013). Overall, implementing digital inclusion programs must empower communities, fight poverty, promote citizenship, and provide better education (Nemer and Reed 2013).

2.2 The Context of Digital India

Computers and computer science as a subject were first introduced to India in the 1990s. By 2014, India had 254.40 million internet subscribers with an internet penetration of 20.39 per 100. But the bleak side of this picture was that 70.23% of them were narrowband subscribers with only 29.77% having an access to a useful connection (Thakore 2018). Only about 40% of the populace has an internet subscription. While many people have digital bank accounts, 90% of all retail transactions in India, by volume, are still made with cash (Singh 2018). E-commerce revenue is growing by more than 25 to 30% per year, yet only 5% of trade in India is done online, compared with 15% in China in 2015 (Kaka et al. 2020).

After the slow sustained growth over the years; it was in 2015 that the current Prime Minister Mr. Narendra Modi launched the ambitious Digital India initiative which aimed to transform India into a digitally empowered society and a knowledge economy. It was an "all-encompassing campaign" with an aim to provide services to the digitally disconnected and underserved sections of society by transforming the prevalent infrastructures into secure and stable digital infrastructure. It had three main facets to it (Vision and vision areas 2015):

1. Access to Digital infrastructure as a core utility service to citizens, ensuring availability of high-speed internet, a lifelong authenticable digital identity, Mobile phone & bank account services, access to Common Service Centre & private space on a public cloud, and cybersecurity
2. Access to digitally-enabled governance (e-governance) and services on demand - The second objective aimed to bring in a seamless integration of cloud-based, real-time government services and making them efficiently, transparently, and reliably accessible to every person through local common service delivery outlets at affordable costs so as to enhance ease of doing business and making financial transactions electronic & cashless for a common man.
3. Universal digital literacy and digital empowerment of citizens – the third facet of Digital India focused on Digital literacy and collaborative digital resources and platforms. It also emphasized on online submission of Govt. documents/certificates and the Availability of digital resources/services in Indian languages.

To make these facets a reality, the Government of India undertook a very extensive methodology of not only laying down standards & policies guidelines for implementation but also provided States the flexibility to identify for inclusion additional state-specific projects, which are relevant for their socio-economic needs. Digital India was further implemented in form of Public-Private Partnerships with successful models to be replicated proactively in other areas.

Appreciating the Digital India program McKinsey (Kaka et al. 2020) reports that "the adoption of key technologies across sectors spurred by the Digital India initiative could help boost India's GDP by $550-billion to $ 1-trillion by 2025". By reducing transaction costs, the program is estimated to create 17 million employment opportunities.

3   Research Methodology

The objective of this study was to evaluate the initiatives undertaken for the digital inclusion of rural communities. The research methodology consisted of two stages – the first stage was to understand the concept of digital inclusion and digital exclusion and the second stage was related to the understanding of the present initiatives undertaken under the Digital India Program for digital inclusion and further the statistical data related to these in Indian Context. For this, initially, the databases such as Ebsco, Proquest, and Google Scholar were searched using keywords like "Digital Inclusion", "Digital Exclusion", "Digital Divide", "Digital Access" etc. further in the context of India. This initially brought forward 92 papers which after the abstract study were shortlisted to 65. These papers were then downloaded for detailed study and only 39 papers were selected as they were found to be most relevant to the research or presented some novel ideas or provided very relevant recommendations to this topic. Content analysis of articles was undertaken to identify and understand the themes, concepts, and framework of Digital inclusion.

Similarly for the second stage analysis, scarcely any research papers were available; hence the government websites and the latest news articles were focused upon and utilized to gather the latest data available in the public domain. The panel data available at various government websites and individual program sites were integrated for analyzing the implementation of these initiatives and build the necessary explanations. Further, the latest reports and studies undertaken by private auditing agencies like Mckinsey, PWC, KPMG, and others were considered and studied. The statistical data related to internet penetration and usage of the launched apps was also collected from the government websites which were available in the public domain to understand the success or failure of the Program.

4   Analysis of the Digital India Rural Initiatives

This section of the study presents the information regarding the various e- initiatives undertaken under the Digital India plan. In addition, it further examines the three aspects of Digital Inclusion as was intended to be achieved under Digital India. Lastly, this section presents a framework of these initiatives which were aimed at rural inclusion.

The plan Digital India was focused on the overall digitization. The initiatives are primarily aimed at both urban and rural populations to include them in the digital mainstream by making more and more governance facilities digitized and digitally connected. But the focus of this section is on the ones that were primarily focused on rural inclusion especially the inclusion of farmers and the digitization of farming-related aspects.

A) Creating Access to Digital Services
The digital infrastructure consisting of availability of telecom, broadband connectivity, computers, and software forms the backbone of the Information Communication and Technology (ICT) sector in a country. Although internet connectivity and per capita connectivity has expanded beyond the traditional urban setup into Tier-II, III, and rural settings, however, India's ICT and digital infrastructure are still ranked low (131) in the ICT development index (Global ICT Development Index 2018).

Thus, one of the first pillars of Digital India was to increase the outreach of digital infrastructure especially in rural areas through Broadband Highway. It aimed electronic delivery of government services to all citizens especially in the far-flung rural areas through extensively increasing the broadband and mobile network penetration for fulfilling this aim of building ICT infrastructure GOI undertook the following initiatives:

Bharat Broadband Network (BBN) was launched as the world's largest rural broadband project having an authorized capital of Rs. 1000 crores. BBN has proved to be instrumental in creating the National Optical Fiber Network (NOFN) which aimed to provide broadband access to 250,000 Gram Panchayats (GPs) (village panchayats) situated in 641 Districts of India through a network of Optical Fiber Cable (Bharat Broadband Network 2015).

The second Pillar of Digital India was the Universal Access to Mobile (UAM). The aim of UAM was to provide mobile internet connectivity to more than 55,600 villages that did not have mobile coverage (Universal access to mobile 2016). Although not a very commercially viable project as villages does not have a wide subscriber base owing to the sparse population, however, this initiative was undertaken for the greater good.

Another aspect of this was the creation of public Wi-Fi hotspots. The Wi-Fi spots were to be created in places likes railway stations in rural areas so to enable citizens to access content without depending on mobile data. In order to meet the global average of one hotspot for every 150 people, this program had the goal of setting up 8 million Wi-Fi hotspots (ASSOCHAM-Deloitte study 2017).

The third pillar focused on providing access was the National Rural Internet Mission and the public internet access program. Under this one of the main projects was the establishment of Common Service Centers (CSC) – a multifunctional end-points for the delivery of government and business services across India especially to provide services in rural areas (CSC 2015).

Common service centers (CSC) special vehicle (SV) scheme was launched to set up 250,000, CSC's across India in each Gram panchayats (village panchayats). These CSC were to be the access points for all the essential public utility-related services such as local education, healthcare, social welfare schemes, financial, and agriculture specific services, other than the B2C services to people in each gram panchayats in rural and remote areas of the country (CSC 2015). At present, it is a pan-India network working for a socially, financially, and digitally inclusive society. CSC's provide some of the following online services in the rural hinterland as the designated digital touch points.

Bharat Bill Pay service through CSC's allows the villagers to electronically pay their water, electricity, gas, DTH, and Phone bills. FASTag is an Electronic Toll Collection system in India. CSC has partnered with the National Highway Authority of India to distribute FASTags through the CSC's network in rural areas (Government to citizen services 2020).

E-passport Seva – CSC has also partnered with the ministry of external affairs to launch Passport Seva services wherein the passport application form can be filled and uploaded. Other services provided include payment of fee as well as taking and scheduling the appointment for visit to the Passport office. Pan Card services - CSCs in collaboration with National Securities Depository Limited (NSDL) are currently providing services for applying for Permanent Account Number (PAN) cards to rural belts (Government to citizen services 2020).

CSC also acts as nodal centers in rural for applying for other healthcare government schemes like Swacch Bharat Abhiyan under which construction of individual household toilets is done as well as Pradhan Mantri Awas Yojana under which affordable housing units are constructed for the poor (Health services 2019). Election commission services – CSC's have partnered with the Election commission of India for delivery of various electoral registration forms and EPIC printing through CSC to ensure hassle-free elections in far lying areas (Government to citizen services 2020).

CSC's also provides financial services at local levels such as GST Suvidha Provider - Goods and Services Tax (GST) is the new system of taxation in India. CSCs across India are the designated help centers for providing GST related services under GST Suvidha (help) Provider scheme. CSC's help the rural merchants not only in filing taxes under GST but also provides the support and necessary training (Financial Inclusion 2020). Insurance facilities - CSC in collaboration with the Insurance Regulatory and Development Authority (IRDA) work are the designated centers for marketing and selling life and non-life insurance products through the Village level entrepreneurs (VLE's) to rural investors. CSC also acts as nodal centers for contributing to The National Pension System (NPS) in rural areas. Pradhan Mantri Fasal Bima Yojana (PMFBY): Crop insurance scheme by the government is also launched through CSC's (Financial Inclusion 2020). CSC's also acts as support centers for Village level entrepreneurs (VLE Bazaar 2016).

Thus for the uninitiated and digitally illiterate rural population, access to all the digitally enable government schemes and services is provided through CSC's. At the same time, village level entrepreneurs are supported in their entrepreneurial efforts and digital education schemes, healthcare schemes are also offered through CSC's. They were also used as study centers for Open school learning. Some of the other online educational courses offered through the CSC's include courses on Basics of IT, English Tally, etc. (Education Services 2018).

Digitization of Post offices and making them Multi-service centers in rural areas was another initiative to increase the infrastructure. The goal was to convert 150,000 Post Offices into multi-service centers to provide services just like CSC in villages where Post offices were already established (Aulakh 2016).

B) Adoption of Digital Services
The second aspect of Digital inclusion is creating an adoption for digital services – making the excluded people literate towards digital technology and ensuring further adoption. GOI under the Digital India Plan launched many sub-programs to create awareness and education for digital initiatives.

NDLM-DISHA program was launched by the Ministry of Communication & Information Technology to provide basic digital literacy to the masses. In the first phase, 10 lakh citizens in each State/UT were targeted covering one person from every digitally illiterate household. Then in the second phase of the program, named Digital Saksharata

Abhiyan (DISHA), the aim was to provide basic digital literacy training to 42.50 lakh citizens including grassroots government functionaries like ASHA and Anganwadi workers and authorized ration dealers (NDLM 2015). Following the successful implementation of the NDLM-DISHA scheme, the new digital literacy scheme 'Pradhan Mantri Gramin Digital Saksharta Abhiyan (PMGDISHA)' was launched by GOI in February 2017. It was focused specifically on the rural population and rural areas of the country. The goal of this scheme was to educate and train at least one member from every digitally unskilled household. Thus the aim was of reaching out to 40% of rural households and training six crore citizens in rural areas through the local CSC's (PMGDISHA 2017).

Cyber Gram Yojana is the program that was launched in 2018 by the Ministry of Minority Affairs to provide basic digital literacy training to students from the minority community, especially girls studying in Madrasas (Muslim Schools) in rural areas (Minority Cybergram Yojana 2018).

Under Digital Finance for Rural India the aim was to create awareness and adoption regarding govt. policies and digital finance options available for rural citizens as well as enabling various mechanisms of digital financial services such as IMPS, UPI, Bank PoS machines, etc. for rural citizens was launched by the government through CSC (Cashless India 2018). CSC centers were also used for delivering and enhancing digital skills.

C) Application of Digital Service Across Rural Sectors

The third part of Digital Inclusion consists of the application of digital initiatives in various sectors and services. Under Digital India Program many initiatives were launched which were available for all citizens of India such as Aadhar (personal identification), E-Biz, E-hospital, E- Pathshala, E- Sampark (connectivity), etc. This study is primarily focused on rural applications hence it discusses specific initiatives that are applicable for farmers and others who form the majority of the rural population. Such rural initiatives have been in areas of education, farming, animal husbandry, health, handicrafts, etc.

In the area of education, the National Institute of Open Schooling (NIOS) and CSC partnered to provide not only facilitation services for NIOS students but also to promote open schooling in rural India, register students, pay registration and examination fee, provide admission status and declare results (NIOS open schooling 2018). Similarly, rural students are being offered online English Speaking Course digitally. CSC has been made the nodal agency for delivering the 'Online English Speaking Course' in partnership with Gurukul Online Learning Solution (GOLS) to provide an education which is targeted at the rural youth to teach them English in a simple and interactive way (Education Services 2018).

In the area of health and medicine, CSC partnered with Apollo Hospitals Limited to offer video-based teleconsultation service in rural belts at affordable rates. In 2016, the CSC program launched its telehealth consultation services throughout India through Allopathic, Homeopathic and Ayurvedic doctors across the country (Health services 2019). Then further on other online health and diagnostic benefits were launched, such as Control-H which is an integrated wireless healthcare monitoring medical device that helps in monitoring Blood Pressure, Heart Rate, Blood Oxygen, body temperature, Total Cholesterol, Haemoglobin, and Blood Glucose and Health Homeo which not only provide teleconsultations but also treatments are provided by world's largest Homoeopathy treatment portal, 'welcomecure.com' (Health services 2019).

For the promotion of rural businesses, VLE Bazaar was launched as an online hand-icrafts market platform in 2016 especially to promote the rural economy and rural craftsmen. It markets unique Indian handicrafts and cottage products which are eth-nic, organic, natural, and handmade. It aims to bridge the gap and provides a common platform between rural artisans and urban consumers. Products procured are the spe-cialty of the particular region with an element of traditional knowledge, local art, and modern technology and design inputs. VLE Bazaar thus not only supports craft-based enterprises but also explore new and commercially sustainable models of livelihood generation in rural belts (VLE Bazaar 2016).

For supporting village-level governance, E-Panchayats, a web portal was launched to provide the entire gamut of e-services to the gram panchayats situated in villages. It helps in e-Governance by automating the functions of Gram Panchayats through the comprehensive software. This portal connects the members of panchayats with the world, empowers the local communities, and helps them in showcasing and sharing their local cultural, social, and economic scenario, their local stories, and their specific challenges (E-panchayat 2020).

To support agriculture directly numerous initiatives were undertaken. For example, ENAM- E-National Agriculture Market (NAM) an India-wide trading portal to unify the national market for agricultural commodities by creating a network of the existing APMC (Agriculture Produce Marketing Committee) mandis was launched. These portals are a one-stop-shop for all APMC services and other related information such as commodity prices, arrivals, buying and selling trade offers, etc. This online market helps in reduc-ing the transaction costs and decreasing the existing information asymmetry (ENAM 2020). Similarly, Farmer Portal was launched to provide pertinent to Agriculture, Ani-mal Husbandry and Fisheries related information as well as important services to the agriculturists and farmers, as well as the private sector. It also shares the data about each sector's production, sales, market rates, daily rates, storage, etc. (Farmer Portal 2015). Because of this portal now the farmers do not need to visit different websites rather information is found at one place itself.

Further, a Fertilizer Monitoring System (FMS) website was launched in 2017 to track the movement of various fertilizers across the supply chain at various stages. This website provides information about the various fertilizers manufacturing companies, their rates, and concessions, their MRP or the market price. It further monitors state-wise product details of movement and availability of fertilizers in different parts of India (Fertilizer Monitoring System 2017). MKisan, an SMS portal was further improved to provide specific, real-time, all-encompassing, and need-based updated information to the farmers across all geographical areas with help of mobile telephony. It not only connects to them and with them but also handles and deals with their queries and concerns (Mkisan 2013).

Considering the increasing reach of the internet and smart phones in rural areas, many mobile apps have been launched to support agricultural and non-agricultural activities.

A Garv Grameen Vidyutikaran App was launched to provide real-time and updated information regarding the electrification in the rural areas and villages, along with information about Government electrification schemes in the rural hinterland (Grameen Vidyutikaran 2015). Agri market portal and supportive App were launched in 2015 to provide the farmers with updated information regarding the latest crop prices to discourage the practices of distress sale which often happens due to information being not available. It works based on mobile GPS technology and captures the location of the farmer and then collects the market pricing information of crops that fall within 50 km of the device owner. (Agrimarket, Crop Insurance mobile app launch 2015).

Another app was Kisan Suvidha, which is a multipurpose mobile app that quickly provides the farmers with the relevant information about the weather, both expected for the current day as well as expected for the next 5 days. It also provides information related to market prices in nearest areas, nearest dealers, agro incubators & advisories, IPM Practices & techniques for plant protection, maximum commodity prices in the state as well as India, and other services. It also provides on-demand services such as extreme weather alerts (Modi launches Kisan Suvidha App 2016). Pusa Krishi app was developed with aim of taking technology to the farm fields. The app is very beneficial for farmers as it helps them in finding easy solutions to various farming & field related problems. It also provides weather alerts and suggests measures to save the crops. It shares information regarding farm machinery and its usage as well as conservation and cultivation practices for increasing the farmer's returns (Govt. launches Pusa Krishi 2016).

Bhuvan Hailstorm App captures the crop loss that has taken place due to a hailstorm. The Agriculture Officer can use this app through their mobile or tablet wherein during their field visit they can capture and upload the photographs of the affected field along with its latitude and longitude. It can further capture information such as the name of the Crop, sources of irrigation, date of sowing, and likely harvesting. This information can then be automatically uploaded to Bhuvan Portal and further plotting and analysis can be done easily for examining loss and further insurance payments (ISRO develops Hailstorm App 2015). Further, for Insurance payments, the Crop Insurance app was launched It can be easily used for calculating the Insurance Premium, the sum insured, premium details, etc. for certain crops and uses parameters such as area, coverage amount and loan amount, etc. for the calculation for a loanee farmer. It can also provide subsidy information of any notified crop in any notified area (Agrimarket, Crop Insurance mobile app launch 2015).

MNCFC app developed by National Remote Sensing Centre, ISRO, was an Android-based application that is useful in gathering field data for crop assessment using satellite imagery in (640 × 480 resolution). It also captures GPS coordinates and information such as crop type, condition, sowing date, soil type, etc. The farmers can also upload pictures taken through their mobile devices. As the data is crowdsourced it will be extremely useful in creating a national geospatial database of crops. As the information can be sent in real-time (Mahalanobis National Crop Forecast Centre 2016).

Intelligent Advisory System for Farmers provides Northeastern Indian farmers with important inputs regarding the five major farming activities (Insect Management, Disease Management, Weed Management, Rice Variety Selection, and Fertilizer Management) which required express advice relating to diagnostic and remedial measures (Intelligent Advisory System for Farmers 2020). Crop Info app provides farmers inputs on production and growing of commercially important Horticultural & Agricultural crops on the user's Smartphone. It provides production aspects, post-harvest technology, processing possibilities, and the latest market information related to the planted crop (Crop Info 2020). PMIS app is for Brinjal & Tomato vegetable crop which is grown at large scale by farmers, are at great risk for crop loss owing to pest infestation. It combines several ecologically safer pest control strategies that help in the reduction of pesticide usage and thus being safe for environmental and human consumption (PMIS Brinjal and Tomato 2020).

In the area of poultry and animal husbandry, the Application for Poultry app was launched. With the help of this app, an applicant who wants to obtain assistance under Poultry Chick and Backyard Poultry Schemes of Govt. of Himachal Pradesh can apply online in the state of Himachal Pradesh (Application for Poultry 2018). Similarly using animal rearers can use the Pashu Poshan app that has been designed to help in cattle rearing. With the help of this software balanced ration is formulated while optimizing the cost considering animal profile, i.e. cattle or buffalo, age, milk production, milk fat, and feeding regime, etc. and milk producers are advised to adjust the quantity of locally available feed ingredients offered to their animals along with mineral mixture (Pashu Poshan 2020).

These have been the most significant initiatives that have been undertaken by the Government of India under Digital India for Digital inclusion of rural hinterland and the farmers. A framework of Digital India initiatives and how they fit into the digital inclusion model is given in Fig. 1.

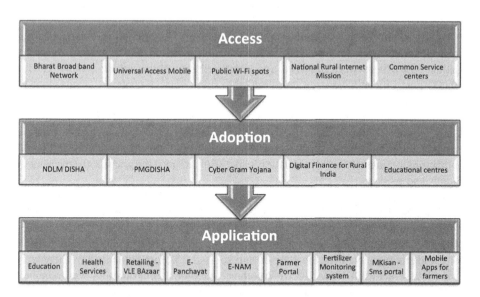

Fig. 1. Framework of digital inclusion under digital India

5   Results and Discussion Regarding the Implementation

The aim of Digital India was to bring the digitally disabled into the mainstream so that they have access to not just internet technologies but also integrated into the new world of immense opportunities and information. The Digital India plan was launched in 2015, since then it has achieved so many milestones and achieved some of the targets with which it was set up. This section presents the statistical data reflecting the numbers achieved so far.

To build the ICT infrastructure GOI had launched Bharat Broadband Network (BBN) to provide broadband connectivity. At present in 2020, so far 4,54,851 km of optical fiber has been laid connecting 1,56,795 g panchayats ensuring connectivity for 13,47,483 rural users (Status of Bharat Net: Bharat Broadband Network 2020).

Similarly, Universal Access to Mobile (UAM) was launched to provide mobile internet connectivity to villages. By the year 2019, 55,699 villages have been connected through mobile networks under this program (India, P. T., 2020, May 08). Another program was to create Public Wi-Fi spots; so far the government has been able to set 31,000 hotspots all over India (Vikaspedia Domains 2020). One of the most successful implementations has been the launch of Common Service Centers (CSC's) for the delivery of government and business services in rural areas. By 2020, more than 250,000 CSC centers have been set up providing services such bill payments, GST- tax services, FASTags for toll collection, applying for passport and pan cards, healthcare facilities, Insurance facilities, Election supportive facilities, Pension contribution facilities, educational facilities and support to local level entrepreneurs. CSC's have proved to be a great success. The data of 2016–17, reveals that almost 2.19 lakh Passport applications while 28.94 lakh Applications for PAN Card was submitted through CSCs (Government to citizen services 2020).

By 2020, almost 36 national and international insurance companies are offering various insurance policies through CSCs (Financial Inclusion 2020). In rural areas, the existing post offices were digitized and converted into multi-service centers. So far 100,000 post offices have been converted into multi-service centers (Government to citizen services 2020).

In the domain of adoption, two prominent programs NDLM-DISHA and Pradhan Mantri Gramin Digital Saksharta Abhiyan (PMGDISHA) were launched to provide digital literacy and digital skills to rural masses to increase the adoption of Digital applications amongst the rural population, especially amongst the grassroots government officials and workers.

Both the programs were very successful, under NDLM-DISHA over 100 lakh citizens have been registered under the scheme for digital literacy of which 87.68 lakh have been trained and 53.46 lakh were certified (Status of PMGDISHA 2020). While under PMGDISHA, 2020, more than 3 lakh centers have been established with 3.67 crore students registered for the courses and so far 2.15 crore students have been certified (Status of PMGDISHA 2020). Another educational program that was launched was Cyberyojana for digital literacy of minority community students especially the girls studying in Madrasas (Muslim Schools). By 2020, 4.52 lakh students have been registered under this program, of which 4.10 lakh students have been trained and 3.22 lakh certified (Cybergram yojana 2020).

To enhance the awareness and adoption of financial digital services the program "Digital Finance for Rural India' was launched. By 2017, CSC's at the local rural level had registered more than 2 crore citizens and provided financial services to around 21 lakh merchants under this educational initiative (Financial Inclusion 2020).

After ensuring the basic infrastructure and digital literacy the next aspect was the practical applications for use of digital technology for the rural economy and rural services. Many web portals and mobile applications were launched to provide information regarding farming, related to education, telehealth and medical services, and online retail and trading portal along with government services.

E-Panchayat, the web portal for e-Governance of panchayats was successfully able to network and automate the functioning of the 2.45 lakh Panchayats in the country (E-panchayat 2020). Similarly, the E-National Agriculture Market (NAM) the government-run trading portal by 2020 was able to network more than 1000 APMC markets in 18 different States & Union Territories (ENAM 2020). While mKisan an SMS portal was able to reach out to more than 50 million farmers through SMS services. More than 24 billion messages related to various aspects of farming have been sent (Status of mKisan 2020).

Other than web portals, a huge number of mobile applications especially useful for farmers was launched and found great success and adoption amongst the farmers. The Agrimarket app which provides the latest local crop prices is being currently used by more than 33000 farmers all over India (Agrimarket App 2020). Similarly, the Kisan Suvidha app which provides weather-related info is being used by 371045 farmers (Kisan Suvidha 2020), while Pusa Krishi which provides farm technology and machinery-related information is being used by 34265 agriculturists in India (Krishi 2020). Crop info app is being used by currently more than 10,000 farmers (Crop Info 2020), while Intelligent Advisory System for Farmers of North East India has found usage amongst 6124 farmers of NE States of India mainly Manipur, Meghalaya (Intelligent Advisory System for Farmers 2020).

Bhuvan Hailstorm app for capturing crop loss due to hailstorms has been used by 1795 farmers to file loss and recovery payments (Bhuvan Hailstorm App 2020), while the crop insurance app has been used by 24777 farmers by 2020 (Crop Insurance 2020).

In the area of poultry and animal husbandry, apps like Application for Poultry have been used for filing 7808 applications as per official records (Application for Poultry 2018), while the Pashu Poshan app specifically for information and advice for dairy farmers have been downloaded and used by more than 50,000 dairy owners (Poshan 2020).

This data in form of the number of consumers of e-services and mobile applications across all three domains of access, adoption, and application clearly reflect the increasing digital inclusion of the rural communities because of Digital India. The results show that in areas of access and digital literacy the numbers are better than in the adoption numbers. Thus Digital India Plan seems to have been able to achieve its aim but if we focus on the total population of 1.33 billion out of which 1 billion is still not digitally connected, these numbers then fall short. It clearly reflects that these numbers of the digitally connected rural population are still very small in relation to the total population which is still digitally excluded. The Digital India plan has not achieved the high results as was expected of this program.

6 Challenges to Digital Inclusion

Digital India aims at the digital inclusion of the digitally illiterate and digitally excluded population of India. A large number of schemes and programs along with Portals, apps, websites have been launched for this inclusion but despite this Digital inclusion seems a faraway dream as it faces many challenges before fulfillment. Although internet penetration and availability is rapidly increasing in India, affordable access to broadband, smart devices, and monthly data packages is required to spread digital literacy. India has one of the cheapest internet data plans in the world, however, nearly 950 million Indians are still without basic internet access (Thakore 2018). This is despite having a steady decline in Smartphone prices with the internet data plans in India being among the cheapest in the world and the average retail price of smart phones steadily declining, connectivity is still out of the reach of nearly 950 million Indians (Kaka et al. 2020).

The initial obstacle is providing access to basic telephony and basic electrification to all the villages. Though the government has initiated a large scale broadband connectivity program but even at present large areas lying in rural belts still lack access to reliable and cheap internet connectivity options.

According to the Socio-Economic Caste Census (SECC) 2011, 73% of households belong to rural India. These rural people are mostly involved in the cultivation and tend to have poor literacy rates and as well as are unaware of the government's schemes and initiatives for their development and upliftment (Raghavan 2016, April 09). This poor literacy rate, lack of knowledge & awareness of government initiatives, and lack of access to ICT lead to Digital Divide and their Digital Exclusion. This is one of the major challenges to Digital inclusion.

Another major challenge is the acceptance of new technologies. For example, digital banking has been easily adopted in urban areas but it is not finding much acceptance in rural India. As per report the IAMAI Mobile internet report 2018 merely 16% of rural users utilize the internet for financial transactions as compared to 44% in the urban areas (IAMAI 2018; Mobile Internet Report 2018). The reasons being not only poor internet connectivity but also because of the lack of the necessary digital literacy to access these online services. Rural people also tend to have distrust and fear of online transactions because of the growing number of cyber attacks. Hence they stay away from being a part of the digital economy.

Another issue is the language barrier. Though the government's digital initiatives have taken care of the services being available in local languages, in fact, more and more apps & websites are providing services in local language for easier understandability of rural people. But even now the majority of banking websites and applications offer services in English which is not understood by them rather they are more comfortable with their regional languages (Banking on future 2019). So focus on local and regional languages is imperative to ensure digital inclusion of rural belts.

Another issue is the delay and slow progress in the development of Digital Infrastructure. Bharat net project has only achieved 50% of its set Target in 2018. Public Penetration of Wi-Fi Spots has also been low (Consultation Paper on Proliferation of Broadband through Public Wi-Fi Networks: TRAI 2016). Projects assigned to PSUs/PSEs are constantly delayed owing to under - skilling, no experience, and technical challenges. RFPs issued by the government are not picked up by the competent private sector owing to their commercial shortcomings and infeasibility (Ray 2018). Thus, these challenges prove to be a great impediment in the digital inclusion of rural belts.

7 The Way Forward

Digital India has made stupendous progress despite the challenges, particularly to the rural population. But for the real Digital inclusion and development of the majority of the population both urban and rural, Digital India still has a long way to go. Digital Inclusion is crucially dependent on a robust and scalable digital infrastructure. Therefore development & enablement of reliable infrastructure requires effective models.

As with the effective PPP and BOT model that has been widely successful in projects such as highways and urban mass rapid transportation projects, similar implementation is required for widening and expanding the digital footprint into the Indian landscape. Higher private participation in the services ecosystem: Effective collaboration with the private sector is critical to the development of the digital infrastructure (Digital India: Unlocking the Trillion Dollar Opportunity 2016). Innovative engagement models that ensure commercial viability, fair and profitable business, and public policy to incentivize the joining of competent private individuals in the digital outreach programs need to be developed jointly through consultation with industry bodies. This will encourage private sector participation and ensure a better response to infrastructure RFPs In addition; startups need to be incentivized for the development of the last mile infrastructure and localized services and applications (Digital Inclusion, GSMA Report 2018).

Existing government infrastructure assets (e.g., post offices, government buildings, CSCs) should be further leveraged for the provision of digital services (Innovate for Digital India 2019). Universal service obligation fund (USOF) under the ministry of communications can be effectively used to incentivize and create a viable business model. The deployment of funds so far has been erratic and not been used to effectively to fund the cost of infrastructure creation in rural areas. Currently, the fund has over INR 451 billion in reserves which can be used to finance rural digital infrastructure growth in India through direct investment or subsidies (ASSOCHAM-Deloitte study 2017).

Satellite communication solutions could be used to speed up broadband access in rural and remote areas. For instance, banks can use VSAT technology to connect remote ATMs, remote branches that need instant access to customer data. It could be used as the last mile connectivity solution in rural areas that lack telecom networks. Another example could be the navigational system NAVIC (Navigation with Indian Constellation), which can have applications in terrestrial, aerial, and marine navigation, disaster management (ANI 2016). Some of the other options for increasing the digital inclusion of rural areas can be:

Improving digital literacy by training the trainer approach can prove to be a successful approach in rural/special areas to increase the adoption of digital services (New Digital Literacy Mission 2018). Further short and crisp E-learning modules can be used over social media outlets to help spread and improve the effectiveness of digital literacy. Digital friendly interactive curriculum must be developed and implemented by the local Educational institutions in rural belts for both students and teachers (How India is inching closer to becoming digitally literate 2019).

Implementing a robust digital governance framework. To keep up with the changing times, just like corporate, the country too should have a Chief Information Officer (CIO) whose responsibility would be to functions as a locus for all parties involved central/state/local government and various private players operating with different technology and administrative levels (AI-backed Digital India 2020). A key role would be the formulation of comprehensive policies & service agreements that ensure technological interoperability of key government functions in rural areas across the country.

One of the top reasons for low adaptability is the complex designs of the service portals and application interfaces (Venkatesh et al. 2014). The IT designers need to understand that Indian rural adopters could be poorly literate in the entire ICT and e-governance ecosystem. Therefore the services and applications need to be user-friendly, visually appealing, and easier to use (Rhonda 2018). There is a strong case to leverage entrepreneurs, technology startups, and students for the development of innovative applications specific to rural populations.

One of the major issues of mistrust of digital technology amongst the rural population is digital security. Hence it is very important to enhance cybersecurity mechanisms. The need of the hour is to establish policies and laws and security mechanisms that ensure the safety of India's cyberspace against threats such as data theft, hacking, cyber-frauds, etc. (Cybersecurity is essential 2020). At the same time communicating and spreading awareness about the security measure to the general population is imperative so to generate trust and confidence amongst them (Singh 2018).

As the Digital India program enters into its fifth year, the focus of execution is now shifted to the rural region and hinterland. We have already started seeing the impact of digital footprint expansion in these areas, especially the tremendous benefits to the agricultural sector and its dependent population. Although it still has a long road ahead, the key is to keep the focus and momentum of efficient delivery and implementation of digital benefits. The transparency and speed that such infrastructure accords are crucial to bringing the country into the 21st century and thereby realizing the long-standing goals of inclusive and sustainable development.

References

Agri market, Crop Insurance mobile app launched for farmers, 23 December 2015. http://www.uniindia.com/agrimarket-crop-insurance-mobile-app-launched-for-farmers/india/news/318070.html. Accessed 29 Sept 29

AI-backed Digital India is the future of e-governance: Nandan Nilekani - ET Government, 02 July 2020. https://government.economictimes.indiatimes.com/news/digital-india/ai-backed-digital-india-is-the-future-of-e-governance-nandan-nilekani/76747911. Accessed 30 Sept 2020

Alam, M.I., Pandey, M., Rautaray, S.S.: A comprehensive survey on cloud computing. Int. J. Inf. Technol. Comput. Sci. 2, 68–79 (2015)

ANI. India's Internet population is likely to touch 600 million by 2020: Study, 05 December 2016. https://www.business-standard.com/article/news-ani/india-s-internet-population-likely-to-touch-600-million-by-2020-study-116120500468_1.html. Accessed 30 Sept 2020

Application for Poultry (2020). https://apps.mgov.gov.in/descp.do?appid=388. Accessed 29 Sept 2020

Aulakh, G.: Government to digitize 1–3 lakh rural post offices by March 2017 (2016). https://eco nomictimes.indiatimes.com/news/politics-and-nation/government-to-digitise-1-3-lakh-rural-post-offices-by-march-2017/articleshow/51255961.cms. Accessed 29 Sept 2020

Banking on the future (2019). https://www2.deloitte.com/content/dam/Deloitte/in/Documents/ financial-services/in-fs-deloitte-banking-colloquium-thoughtpaper-cii.pdf. Accessed 30 Sept 2020

Bharat Broadband Network (2015). http://www.bbnl.nic.in/index1.aspx?lsid=570&lev=2&lid= 467&langid=1. Accessed 29 Sept 2020

Bhuvan Hailstorm App (2020). https://mkisan.gov.in/downloadmobileapps.aspx/bhuvan. Accessed 29 Sept 2020

Bonilla, M.H., Pretto, N.: Inclusão Digital: Polêmica Contemporânea. EDUFBA, Salvador (2011)

Bradbrook, G., Fisher, J.: Digital Equality: Reviewing Digital Inclusion Activity and Mapping the Way Forwards. CitizensOnline, London (2004)

Brotcorne, P.: A theoretical revision of the evolution of the concept of digital inclusion (2016)

Campos-Castillo, C.: Revisiting the first-level digital divide in the United States: gender and race/ethnicity patterns, 2007–2012. Soc. Sci. Comput. Rev. **33**, 423–439 (2015). https://doi.org/10.1177/0894439314547617

Cashless India (2018). http://cashlessindia.gov.in/schemes.html. Accessed 12 Sept 2020

Consultation Paper on Proliferation of Broadband through Public Wi-Fi Networks: TRAI, July 2016. https://www.mygov.in/sites/default/files/mygov_1468492162190667.pdf. Accessed 30 Sept 2020

Correa, T.: Literature Review: Understanding the "Second Level Digital Divide" (2008). http:// utexas.academia.edu/TeresaCorrea/

Correa, T., Pavez, I.: Digital inclusion in rural areas: a qualitative exploration of challenges faced by people from isolated communities. J. Comput.-Mediat. Commun. **21**(3), 247–263 (2016)

Correa, T., Pavez, I., Contreras, J.: Beyond access: a relational and resource-based model of household Internet adoption in isolated communities. Telecommun. Policy **41**(9), 757–768 (2017). https://doi.org/10.1016/j.telpol.2017.03.008

Correa, T., Pavez, I., Contreras, J.: Digital inclusion through mobile phones? A comparison between mobile-only and computer users in internet access, skills, and use. Inf. Commun. Soc. **23**(7), 1074–1091 (2020)

Crop Info (2020). https://cropinfo.in/agriinfo/mobile-applications/. Accessed 29 Sept 2020

Crop Insurance (2020). https://digitalindia.gov.in/content/crop-insurance-mobile-app. Accessed 29 Sept 2020

CSC (2015). https://csc.gov.in/index.php?option=com_content&view=article&id=174&Ite mid=331. Accessed 29 Sept 2020

Cybersecurity is essential for Digital India initiatives - ET Government, 03 April 2020. https://government.economictimes.indiatimes.com/news/digital-india/cyber-security-is-essential-for-digital-india-initiatives/74964681. Accessed 30 Sept 2020

Cybergram yojana (2020). http://www.cybergramyojana.in/overview-of-cybergram-yojana.html. Accessed 27 Sept 2020

Digital Inclusion, GSMA Report (2018). http://www.gsma.com/mobilefordevelopment/wp-con tent/uploads/2018/11/GSMA_DigitalInclusion-Report_Web_Singles_2.pdf. Accessed 30 Sept 2020

Digital India: Unlocking The Trillion Dollar Opportunity (2016). https://www2.deloitte.com/con tent/dam/Deloitte/in/Documents/technology-media-telecommunications/in-tmt-digital-india-unlock-opportunity-noexp.pdf. Accessed 30 Sept 2020

Education Services (2018). https://csc.gov.in/education. Accessed 27 Sept 2020

Ekbia, H.R.: Digital inclusion and social exclusion: the political economy of value in a networked world. Inf. Soc. **32**(3), 165–175 (2016)

ENAM (2017). https://enam.gov.in. Accessed 28 Sept 2020

E-panchayat (2020). https://panchayatonline.gov.in/globalSaveRegister.htm. Accessed 29 Sept 2020

Ewing, D.L., Monsen, J.J., Kielblock, S.: Teachers' attitudes towards inclusive education: a critical review of published questionnaires. Educ. Psychol. Pract. **34**, 150–165 (2018). https://doi.org/10.1080/02667363.2017.1417822

Farmer Portal (2015). https://farmer.gov.in/. Accessed 28 Sept 2020

Fertilizer Monitoring System (2017). https://digitalindia.gov.in/content/fertiliser-monitoring-system-fms. Accessed 28 Sept 2020

Financial Inclusion (2020). https://csc.gov.in/financialinclusion. Accessed 28 Sept 2020

Global ICT Development Index (2018). https://www.itu.int/net4/ITU-D/idi/2017/index.html. Accessed 25 Sept 2020

Goggin, G., et al.: Digital Inclusion: An International Comparative Analysis. Rowman & Littlefield, Lanham (2018)

Government to citizen services (2020). https://www.csc.gov.in/governmenttocitizen. Accessed 25 Sept 2020

Govt. launches Pusa Krishi app, 21 March 2016. https://timesofindia.indiatimes.com/city/delhi/Govt-launches-mobile-app-Pusa-Krishi/articleshow/51498159. Accessed 23 Sept 2020

Vidyutikaran, G. (2015). https://digitalindia.gov.in/content/garv-grameen-vidyutikaran-mobile-app. Accessed 28 Sept 2020

Gray, T.J., Gainous, J., Wagner, K.M.: Gender and the digital divide in Latin America. Soc. Sci. Q. **98**(1), 326–340 (2017)

Hargittai, E., Hinnant, A.: Digital inequality: differences in young adults' use of the internet. Commun. Res. **35**(5), 602–621 (2008)

Health services (2019). https://csc.gov.in/health. Accessed 28 Sept 2020

How India is inching closer to becoming digitally literate (2019). https://yourstory.com/2019/06/national-digital-literacy-mission/. Accessed 30 Sept 2020

IAMAI 2018 Mobile Internet Report (2018). https://cms.iamai.in/Content/ResearchPapers/2b08cce4-e571-4cfe-9f8b-86435a12ed17.pdf. Accessed 1 Oct 2020

India Exclusion report (2017). https://www.defindia.org/wp-content/uploads/2017/07/India-Exclusion-Report-2017_Low-Res.pdf. Accessed 20 Sept 2020

ASSOCHAM-Deloitte study: India needs 80 lakhs of Wi-Fi hotspots, 12 January 2017. https://www.assocham.org/newsdetail.php?id=6139. Accessed 30 Sept 2020

India, P.T.: 55,669 villages to have mobile connectivity by 2019, 08 May 2020. https://www.india.com/news/india/55669-villages-to-have-mobile-connectivity-by-2019-1168919/. Accessed 25 Sept 2020

Innovate for Digital India (2019). http://innovatefordigitalindia.intel.in/indiadigital.html. Accessed 30 Sept 2020

Intelligent Advisory System for Farmers (2020). https://www.cdac.in/index.aspx?id=aboutus_farmers. Accessed 27 Sept 2020

ISRO develops Hailstrom App, 5 October 2018. https://www.thehindu.com/news/national/isro-develops-hailstrom-app-to-assess-crop-damage/article7726309.ece. Accessed 26 Sept 2020

Kaka, N., et al.: Digital India: technology to transform a connected nation, 01 June 2020. https://www.mckinsey.com/business-functions/mckinsey-digital/our-insights/digital-india-technology-to-transform-a-connected-nation. Accessed 5 Oct 2020

Katz, V.S.: What it means to be 'under-connected' in lower-income families. J. Child. Media **11**(2), 241–244 (2017). https://doi.org/10.1080/17482798.2017.1305602

Letch, N., Carroll, J.: Towards anticipating IS consequences: an anatomy of socio-technical interaction networks (STINs). In: ACIS 2008 Proceedings, p. 63 (2008)

Leung, L.: Availability, access, and affordability across 'digital divides': common experiences amongst minority groups. J. Telecommun. Digit. Econ. **2**(2), 38 (2014)

Livingstone, S., Helsper, E.: Gradations in digital inclusion: children, young people, and the digital divide. New Media Soc. **9**(4), 671–696 (2007)

Mahalanobis National Crop Forecast Centre (2016). https://www.ncfc.gov.in/index.html. Accessed 9 Sept 2020

Mkisan (2013). https://mkisan.gov.in/. Accessed 11 Sept 2020

Minority Cybergram Yojana (2018). https://www.defindia.org/minority-cyber-gram-yojana/. Accessed 11 Sept 2020

Modi launches Kisan Suvidha App, 21 Match 2016. https://inc42.com/flash-feed/narendra-modi-kisan-suvidha-app/. Accessed 28 Sept 2020

NDLM (2015). https://dibsindian.com/ndlm.htm. Accessed 2 Sept 2020

Nemer, D., Reed, P.: Can a community technology center be for profit? A case study of LAN Houses in Brazil. In: Proceedings of the CIRN 2013 Community Informatics Conference, Prato, Italy (2013)

Nemer, D., Reed, P.: Can a community technology center be for-profit? A case study of LAN houses in Brazil. In: CIRN 2013 Community Informatics Conference, pp. 1–9, October 2013

New Digital Literacy Mission aims to train 60 million from rural India, 27 June 2018. http://www.hindustantimes.com/tech/new-digital-literacymission-aims-to-train-60-million-from-rural-india/story-6zcSUJvxAYHpgjrKz1fRFP.html. Accessed 30 Sept 2020

Newman, L., Browne-Yung, K., Raghavendra, P., Wood, D., Grace, E.: Applying a critical approach to investigate barriers to digital inclusion and online social networking among young people with disabilities. Inf. Syst. J. **27**(5), 559–588 (2017)

NIOS open schooling (2018). https://digitalseva.csc.gov.in/web/services/education. Accessed 27 Sept 2020

Notley, T.: Young people, online networks, and social inclusion. J. Comput. Mediat. Commun. **14**(4), 1208–1227 (2009)

Poshan, P. (2020). https://hi.vikaspedia.in/agriculture/animal-husbandry. Accessed 29 Sept 2020

Pearce, K.E., Rice, R.E.: Digital divides from access to activities: comparing mobile and personal computer Internet users. J. Commun. **63**, 721–744 (2013). https://doi.org/10.1111/com.2013.63.issue-4

PMGDISHA (2017). https://www.pmgdisha.in/about-pmgdisha/. Accessed 27 Sept 2020

PMIS Brinjal, Tomato (2020). https://mkisan.gov.in/downloadmobileapps.aspx. Accessed 29 Sept 2020

Krishi, P. (2020). http://pusakrishi.iari.res.in/. Accessed 3 Oct 2020

Raghavan, T.S.: 73 percent of households live in rural India (2016, April 09). https://www.thehindu.com/news/national/73-households-live-in-rural-india-socioeconomic-and-caste-census/article7382614.ece. Accessed 30 Sept 2020

Ray, R.K.: A third of PSU infrastructure projects were delayed, cost overrun up at 19.7%, 22 March 2018. https://www.financialexpress.com/archive/a-third-of-psu-infrastructure-projects-delayed-cost-overrun-up-at-197/1234934/. Accessed 15 Sept 2020

Rhonda, Z.: Picture online open access program and meeting document digital inclusion for low-skilled and low-literate people: a landscape review, 23 July 2018. https://unesdoc.unesco.org/ark:/48223/pf0000261791. Accessed 18 Sept 2020

Roberts, E., Beel, D., Philip, L., Townsend, L.: Rural resilience in a digital society. J. Rural Stud. **54**, 355–359 (2017)

Robinson, L., et al.: Digital inequalities and why they matter. Inf. Commun. Soc. **18**, 569–582 (2015). https://doi.org/10.1080/1369118X.2015.1012532

Rose, N., Seton, C., Tucker, J., van der Zwan, R.: Digital and included: Empowering social housing communities. In the Regional Initiative for Social Innovation and Research (RISIR). Southern Cross University, Coffs Harbour (2014). http://www.academia.edu/download/42993483/Digital_and_Included_Empowering_Social_H20160223-14774-gcnjwh.pdf

Selwyn, N., Facer, K.: Beyond the Digital Divide: Rethinking Digital Inclusion for the 21st Century (Futurelab). Slough, Egyesült Királyság, Bristol (2007)

Singh, S.: How safe is digital India? 14 January 2018. https://economictimes.indiatimes.com/news/economy/policy/how-safe-is-digital-india-indias-vast-data-pools-need-to-be-secured-with-tighter-de-risking-tools/articleshow/62489823.cms?from=mdr. Accessed 30 Sept 2020

Status Kisan Suvidha (2020). https://www.kisansuvidha.com/. Accessed 7 Nov 2020

Status of Agrimarket App (2020). https://digitalindia.gov.in/content/agrimarket-app. Accessed 10 Nov 2020

Status of Bharat Net: Bharat Broadband Network (2020). http://www.bbnl.nic.in/index1.aspx?lsid=570&lev=2&lid=467&langid=1. Accessed 12 Nov 2020

Status of ENAM (2020). https://enam.gov.in/web/eNamcoverage. Accessed 2 Nov 2020

Status of mKisan (2020). https://mkisan.gov.in/. Accessed 14 Nov 2020

Status of PMGDISHA (2020). https://pmgdisha.in. Accessed 12 Nov 2020

Sum, S., Mathews, R.M., Hughes, I., Campbell, A.: Internet use and loneliness in older adults. Cyberpsychol. Behav. 11(2), 208–211 (2008)

Thakore, A.: What is digital Inclusion? And is my digital India immersing in It?, 30 June 2018. https://digitalequality.in/digital-inclusion-definitions-and-status-in-india/

Townsend, L., Sathiaseelan, A., Fairhurst, G., Wallace, C.: Enhanced broadband access as a solution to the social and economic problems of the rural digital divide. Local Econ. 28(6), 580–595 (2013)

Universal access to mobile (2016). https://digitalindia.gov.in/content/universal-access-mobile-connectivity. Accessed 29 Sept 2020

van Dijk, J.: Digital divide research, achievements, and shortcomings. Poetics 34(45), 221235 (2006)

Venkatesh, V., Sykes, T.A., Venkatraman, S.: Understanding e-Government portal use in rural India: the role of demographic and personality characteristics. Inf. Syst. J. 24(3), 249–269 (2014)

Vikaspedia Domains (2020). https://vikaspedia.in/e-governance/digital-india/public-wi-fi-hot spots. Accessed 26 Sept 2020

Vision and Vision Areas: Digital India Programme: Ministry of Electronics & Information Technology (MeitY) Government of India (2015). https://digitalindia.gov.in/content/vision-and-vision-areas. Accessed 4 Sept 2020

VLE Bazaar (2016). https://vlebazaar.csc.gov.in/. Accessed 12 Sept 2020

Walton, P., Kop, T., Spriggs, D., Fitzgerald, B.: Digital Inclusion (2013)

Warschauer, M.: Technology and Social Inclusion: Rethinking the Digital Divide. MIT Press, Cambridge (2004)

Willis, S., Tranter, B.: Beyond the 'digital divide' Internet diffusion and inequality in Australia. J. Sociol. 42(1), 43–59 (2006)

World Development Report 2018. https://www.worldbank.org/en/publication/wdr2018. Accessed 29 Sept 2020

Dealing with the Challenge of Business Analyst Skills Mismatch in the Fourth Industrial Revolution

Denise Mukozho and Lisa F. Seymour(✉) ⓘ

CITANDA, Department of IS, University of Cape Town, Cape Town, South Africa
MKZDEN001@myuct.ac.za, Lisa.seymour@uct.ac.za

Abstract. This paper describes the skills mismatch within the Business Analysis profession. The Business Analysis profession emerged in the early 90s and is still considered a new field in the information systems domain which has not been extensively researched. However, the advent of the Fourth Industrial Revolution has put the future skills of the profession into question. This paper uses the Business Analysis Competency Model to develop a proposed Skills Mismatch framework to understand the skills mismatch within the Business Analysis profession. The Business Analysis Competency Model highlights technical skills, business skills, analysis techniques, interpersonal skills, and the Business Analysis Methodology. The gap identified in the literature is that there are limited studies in the digital age that have tracked the changes in required skills over time. This paper will be useful to the Business Analysis Body of Knowledge by proposing a framework for addressing a possible Fourth Industrial Revolution induced skills mismatch.

Keywords: Skills mismatch · Business analyst · Fourth industrial revolution · Skills

1 Introduction

Technology is advancing at a rapid pace and the world has undergone numerous transitions in technological advancements which are commonly referred to as "Industrial revolutions". The Fourth Industrial Revolution (4IR) is defined as the "revolutionary change that occurs when Information Technology (IT) proliferates in all industries, that is, the primary, secondary, and tertiary industries" [1]. The 4IR is projected to make obsolete certain skills and create a mismatch between the current and future skills [2]. The 4IR is also predicted to result in significant job losses, automation of processes, and reduced need for human labour. Low skilled labour is mostly affected however high skilled labour will not be spared. The Business Analysis profession is impacted which may result in skills mismatch [3].

This paper firstly introduces the Business Analyst (BA) role and context. It then focuses on describing the current Business Analyst skills and those required for the 4IR and the disparities between them. The Business Analysis Competency model and factors that could reduce the mismatch are used to develop the proposed Skills Mismatch conceptual framework.

© Springer Nature Switzerland AG 2021
A. Garimella et al. (Eds.): WeB 2020, LNBIP 418, pp. 111–120, 2021.
https://doi.org/10.1007/978-3-030-79454-5_10

2 Business Analysis

According to the International Institute of Business Analysis [4], business analysis is "the practice of enabling change in an organisational context, by defining needs and recommending solutions that deliver value to stakeholders." Paul and Tan [5] view business analysis as the bridge between business and IT. Yet the definition of the role of a BA is elusive resulting in confusion of the title, role, skills and required knowledge of a BA [6]. The business systems analyst, functional analyst, and systems analyst are all being employed in this role [7]. Not only is the position of the BA ambiguous, so are the skills, and competencies required for the job [8]. This lack of an agreed definition of the role of a BA creates conflicting skills expectations, a gap that requires further exploration.

2.1 Historical Context

The BA profession is a relatively young profession that developed in the 1990s and there is little evidence of its longevity [5]. Research has found that the business/systems analysts' skill requirements show the greatest change in longitudinal studies [6]. There is limited recognition within the academic community and little research that has been conducted into the historical BA skills and competencies.

2.2 Current Context

BAs play a pivotal role in the organisational success of any business [5]. The body of knowledge asserts that the need for BAs is predicted to increase in the future with an increase in technological developments [7, 9]. Yet the "BA profession is characterised by constant change and uncertainty, placing pressure on BAs to regularly update their skills"[10].

3 Business Analysis Skills

Park and Jeong [9] describe a skill as the ability one has, to perform a given task, achieve the recommended results using a related given amount of time and power. This is sometimes split into context general and context-specific skills [11]. The BA role definition is not consistent in literature [11]. Hence support for ascertaining the skills needed to fulfil the role has been expressed [6]. The Business Analysis Competency Model comprises domain, technical, business, and soft skills [9]. The IIBA have outlined the key competencies and techniques relevant for a BA and these are summarized in Table 1. They will now be described.

Table 1. BA competency model [12].

IIBA Business Analysis Competency Model			
Underlying Competencies	Knowledge Areas	Techniques	Proficiency Scale
• Tools and Technology • Analytical Thinking and Problem-Solving Behavioural Characteristics • Business Knowledge • Communication Skills • Interaction Skills	• Solution Evaluation • Business Analysis Planning and Monitoring • Elicitation and Collaboration • Requirements Lifecycle Management • Strategy Analysis • Requirements Analysis and Design Definition	• Agile • Information Technology • Business Architecture • Business Process Management • Business Intelligence • Business Data Analytics • Cybersecurity	• General Awareness • Practical Knowledge • Skilled • Expert • Strategist

3.1 Technical Skills

Technical skills are the ability to use technology tools and the technical knowledge surrounding the hardware, software and programming required to develop new or modified information [8, 13]. Technical skills entail specialised knowledge or a set of abilities that allows one to perform practical work and varies across industries such as science and IS [14]. There are two opposing thoughts in the literature on the need for technical skills; the first thought is that the BA professional must have technical skills due to the rapid pace of change while the second thought is that, advances in computer technology will lessen the need for technical expertise [15]. In their study of the IS industry between 2013 and 2018, Tan et al. [16] found that the need for technical skills remains high. BAs must therefore have technical skills to be successful in their role [9]. Recent technological advances require organisations to rethink the BA role [17]. IS services are highly technical, therefore technical skills are likely to remain relatively important [18].

3.2 Business Skills

Evans [8] defines business skills as "broad knowledge of business practices and knowledge of different functional areas within the organisation", and McGuinness et al. [13] extend the definition to include "the knowledge about the organisation's business processes". Business skills identified included business case development, stakeholder engagement and management, industry knowledge, business problem analysis and IS strategy evaluation [5, 16]. This matches with the IIBA competency model to a certain extent as BAs are expected to have knowledge in the Business domain as part of the requirements gathering process [6]. The position of an all-rounder BA who has overall business knowledge has research support [11].

3.3 Analysis Skills and Techniques

McGuinness et al. [13] describe analysis techniques as the application of knowledge management skills and methodologies in solving complex problems. BAs are responsible for "transferring requirements or information from users and developers, facilitating their ideas" [9]. In prior research [5] the ability to apply professional analytical techniques was highlighted as critical to the success of a BA [5]. This included requirements elicitation, business systems/processes modelling, and solution design.

3.4 Interpersonal Skills

Interpersonal skills relate to an individual's behaviours and attitudes, interpersonal communication, and group behaviour. Researchers opine that BAs must put the highest degree of importance in behavioural skills such as communication, negotiation, ability to challenge, and problem-solving, as these skills are critical in development teams [5, 8, 19]. Interpersonal skills have been viewed to be top skills and traits for entry-level IS workers as well as critical for the BA professional [14, 20]. Personal characteristics are perceived as "more valuable than technical skills and interpersonal skills and personal traits are more valuable than technical skills and organisational knowledge" [6].

3.5 Methodological Skills

The BA profession has been characterised by an evolution of the ways of work. The perception of the BA role is that of a professional that may be tasked with different activities from one project to another [21]. There is currently a transition from a single domain BA employing the waterfall-based delivery method towards a cross-functional multi-skilled BA working on an agile delivery methodology [16]. The dominant theme for the BA profession is an individual who can be adaptable to using different methodologies such as Waterfall, Agile, Lean, Six Sigma etc.

3.6 Skills Weightings

There are conflicting viewpoints in the literature with regards to the criticality of the relevant BA skill categories. There are varying opinions with some scholars advocating for technical skills for IS professionals to be successful in the workplace [6]. Aasheim et al. [20] argue that interpersonal skills rank highly in literature based on the assumption that the foundational technical skills have not changed over time. Tan et al. [16] found that the need for technical skills remains high, whilst business knowledge requirements remain relatively low. Other researchers have seen an almost equal requirement for both technical and business skills and in certain instances where non-technical skills are preferred [9]. Recent technological advances and the shift anticipated from the 4IR require organisations to rethink the roles and responsibilities of IS professionals [17]. BAs must be fluent in both business and technical language while having a good dose of interpersonal skills. This contradicts studies where BAs have been placed in either a purely business or technical role [22].

4 Business Analysis Skills for the 4IR

There are different thoughts about the 4IR. One opinion is that the 4IR is not different from other revolutions but a step-change in the evolution journey the same way that the digital computer impacted the third industrial revolution [20]. Few professions in human history have advanced as rapidly as the IS profession has in the last several decades. Taking into consideration the advancement in technology, Matthee and Turpin [23] recommend the importance of problem-solving and critical thinking as essential 21st-century skills; however, these skills have been a requirement since the inception of the BA career. Another opinion positions the 4IR as a unique revolution due to its nature, with possible impacts on BA skills resulting in a skills mismatch. In the 4IR there is a greater emphasis on integration, interoperability, application architecture and data architecture [20].

The 4IR demands new and faster ways of work including a more technical focused BA as the technological complexity increases. The top three technical skills sought out for the 4IR are Cloud Computing, Big Data, and Security [24]. According to Birgit et al. [25] "technological innovations will be drivers for the transformation of the labour market over the next decade, the innovations will transform industries and business models, change required skills, and shorten the shelf-life of employees' existing skill sets".

Research notes that IS professionals will face challenges in assimilating the ever-increasing amount of new knowledge in the field [21]. BAs must prepare for the challenges that the 4IR will present. Furthermore, the core IS competencies are noted to remain relevant in the 4IR [23]. However, scholars note that there will be a BA skills shortage and business skills gap in the IS workforce [16]. This aligns with researchers such as Birgit et al. [25] who forecast a possible mismatch as the skill sets needed to fulfil future jobs still need to be developed. This notion corresponds with other scholars who have noted the fluidity of the IS field and the need to constantly update skills [26]. Hahm [26] measured the following variables: the attitudes of workers to the 4IR, the importance of skills, intention to use, belief in improvement, efficacy to use, and negative cognition noting these variables play a role in determining how workers will perform in the 4IR era. Table 2 outlines and contrasts identified current and future BA skills.

Mismatch refers to a "misalignment between the composition of labour demand and labour supply" [27]. According to McGuinness [13] a mismatch occurs when there is "overskilling, underskilling, horizontal mismatch, or through the underutilization of skills and the skill gaps". Studies note that in the 4IR novel jobs will require different skills and redeploying to the new ways of work will exacerbate the skill mismatch [28]. It is difficult to predict the type of 4IR skills as the rate of change is not following a straight predictable line, however, there is a sense of agreement in both literature and in practice that the current skills will not be adequate for the era and that the 4IR will cause structural changes and result in a skills mismatch [29].

Table 2. Current and future BA skills. Compiled from literature [30–33]

Skills Category	Current	Future
Technical	<ul><li>Knowledge of Operating systems and applications</li><li>Testing Skills</li><li>Programming languages</li><li>Database</li><li>Software development understanding</li><li>Business intelligence and reporting software</li><li>Data mining</li><li>Data visualisation</li></ul>	<ul><li>Business intelligence and reporting software</li><li>Data mining</li><li>Data visualisation</li><li>Cybersecurity</li><li>Internet of Things</li><li>Artificial Intelligence</li><li>Automated Testing</li></ul>
Business	<ul><li>Finance and the economy</li><li>Business case development</li><li>Domain knowledge</li><li>Subject matter expertise</li><li>Organisation structures and design</li><li>Supplier management</li><li>Waste reduction</li><li>Experimentation</li></ul>	
Interpersonal	<ul><li>Communication</li><li>Relationship building</li><li>Influencing</li><li>Teamwork</li><li>Political awareness</li><li>Analytical skills and critical thinking</li><li>Attention to detail</li><li>Problem solving</li><li>Leadership</li><li>Self-belief</li></ul>	
Methodology	<ul><li>Waterfall Model</li><li>Agile Software Development</li></ul>	<ul><li>Agile Software Development</li><li>DevOps</li><li>Six Sigma</li><li>Lean</li></ul>
Analytical Techniques and Skills	<ul><li>Business Process Modelling Notation</li><li>Artifacts/Documentation</li><li>UML</li><li>Project management</li></ul>	<ul><li>Design Thinking</li><li>Lean start-up</li><li>Iterative Agile Build</li><li>Actual Products/Working software</li><li>Understanding the customer</li><li>Increasing the value of features to the customer</li></ul>

5   Proposed Business Analysis Skills Mismatch Framework

Figure 1 outlines the proposed framework for this paper derived from the Business Analysis Competency Model. Literature suggests that due to various factors, the 4IR may induce a skills mismatch between the current and the future 4IR BA skill sets. Variables such as attitude toward the 4IR, education, lifelong learning, and cross-functionality have been proposed to address the mismatch. A quantitative methodology will be used to study the proposed framework. The study will be conducted in the South African context using an online survey to gather the data from Business Analysts. Due to the Covid-19 pandemic and social distancing requirements, convenience sampling may be utilised as a method to target the relevant sample population [34]. Inferential statistics such as non-parametric ranking tests, comparison of means may be performed on the received data responses within and between the 'current' and 'future' skills categories to compare ranking of a particular skill. Within a category, the skills will be ranked in terms of importance from the most important to least important and the overall weighting of each skill will be derived from the rankings. The difference in ranking of skills may reveal a skills mismatch when the ranking of a skill in the current is different to the ranking in the 4IR.

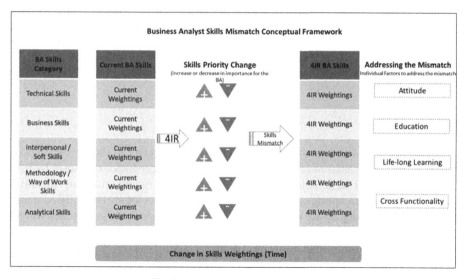

Fig. 1. Skills mismatch framework

5.1 Education

Researchers [19] posit that studies must identify the "skills that BAs indicate as important for their jobs so they can acquire essential training". It is necessary for the BA to get a comprehensive set of skills [35]. In the rapidly changing field of IS, educational programs must be continually re-evaluated and revised to meet the 4IR requirements[20]. Trauth et al. [15] assert that there is an "expectation gap" between industry needs and academic preparation. Industry and academic institution must work together to close this gap by ensuring that academic programmes proactively react to the 4IR trends skills requirements [25].

5.2 Lifelong Learning

The BA must establish a culture of lifelong learning to cope with new demands from the 4IR environment [36]. There is a need for continued learning throughout an IS worker's career by involving themselves in several short courses to keep their knowledge up to date. Several BA courses have expiry dates and/or require regular renewal which gives the BA an opportunity to refresh their skills with updated knowledge and skills. Going forward "IS students and professionals must show a willingness to learn and constantly be learning due to the constant changes in IS" [20].

5.3 Cross Functionality

The BA must break away from the traditional/confined role specific duties and become versatile in their contribution to the business [37] as well as begin to focus on 4IR key specialisations such as cyber security and data analytics. The BA must be agile and adaptable to the new ways of work [38] and with the rate of change of technology prepare themselves for a changing professional landscape. Domain expertise will become increasingly important, and gradually there is a trend of BAs doubling up as a domain expert and as BAs [21]. Researchers are advocating for cross functionality within IS teams to maximise their output which may impact the traditional requirements focused role of the BA [39].

5.4 BA Attitudes

Success in the 4IR will depend largely on how well BAs adapt to these new ways of working, setting up teams, and using group collaboration, Acceptance of change by BAs is crucial for the 4IR to be able to adapt and succeed in a rapidly changing situation. BAs who are more accepting of change have a higher chance of successfully adapting to it and therefore reducing the skills mismatch. People who have these attitudes will be more adaptable and likely to achieve higher performance in the 4IR era [26]. There is a need for a positive attitude and motivation in the IS field.

6 Conclusion

The aim of this paper was to review current and 4IR BA skills by reviewing existing literature. The paper found that there will be a strong bias towards interpersonal and technical BA skills in the 4IR with key focus on cross functionality. The paper proposed a framework for addressing a possible 4IR induced skills mismatch. The identified gap in the literature is limited longitudinal studies tracking the change in importance of BA skills and a lack of understanding of the required skills for the 4IR. There are contradictions in the literature as there were varying opinions on which skills will be relevant for the BA. Hence further research is needed to address this. Further empirical studies will be vital to inform the BA Body of Knowledge and to assist BAs in ensuring that their skills are matched for the 4IR.

References

1. Lee, M., et al.: How to respond to the fourth industrial revolution, or the second information technology revolution? Dynamic new combinations between technology, market, and society through open innovation. J. Open Innov. Technol. Mark. Complexity **4**, 21 (2018)
2. World Economic Forum. The Future of Jobs Report. Cologny-Geneva, pp. 3–26 (2016)
3. Manyika, J.: Technology, jobs, and the future of work, McKinsey Global Institute (2017). https://www.mckinsey.com/featured-insights/employment-and-growth/technology-jobs-and-the-future-of-work. Accessed 07 Mar 2021
4. IIBA. What is Business Analysis? (2021). https://www.iiba.org/professional-development/career-centre/what-is-business-analysis/. Accessed 07 Mar 2021
5. Paul, D., Tan, Y.L.: An investigation of the role of business analysts in IS development. In: ECIS 2015 Completed Research Papers (2015)
6. Richards, D., Marrone, M.: Identifying the education needs of the business analyst: an Australian study. Aust. J. Inf. Syst. **18** (2014)
7. Vongsavanh, A., Campbell, B.: The roles and skill sets of systems vs business analysts. In: ACIS 2008 Proceedings, pp. 1059–1068 (2008)
8. Evans, N.: The need for an analysis body of knowledge (ABOK) - will the real analyst please stand up? Issues Inf. Sci. Inf. Technol. **1**, 313 (2004)
9. Park, J., Jeong, S.R.: A study on the relative importance of underlying competencies of business analysts. KSII Trans. Internet Inf. Syst. **10**, 3986–4007 (2016)
10. Misic, M.M., Graf, D.K.: Systems analyst activities and skills in the new millennium. J. Syst. Softw. **71**, 31–36 (2004)
11. Vashist, R., McKay, J., Marshall, P.J.: The roles and practices of business analysts: a boundary practice perspective. In: International Conference on Information Systems (2010)
12. IIBA. Business Analysis Competency Model 4.0 (2021). https://www.iiba.org/professional-development/business-analysis-competency-model/. Accessed 07 Mar 2021
13. McGuinness, S., Pouliakas, K., Redmond, P.: Skills mismatch: concepts, measurement and policy approaches. J. Econ. Surv. **32**, 985–1015 (2018)
14. Todd, P.A., McKeen, J.D., Gallupe, R.B.: The evolution of IS job skills: a content analysis of IS job advertisements from 1970 to 1990. MIS Q. **19**, 1–27 (1995)
15. Trauth, E.M., Farwell, D.W., Lee, D.M.S.: The IS expectation gap: industry expectations versus academic preparation. MIS Q. **17**, 293–307 (1993)
16. Tan, Y.L., Nakata, K., Paul, D.: Aligning IS master's programs with industry. J. Inf. Syst. Educ. **29**, 169–182 (2018)
17. Jones, K., Leonard, L., Lang, G.: Desired skills for entry level IS positions: identification and assessment. J. Comput. Inf. Syst. **58**, 214–220 (2018)
18. Branchet, B., Sanseau, P.: From technical to non-technical skills among information systems suppliers. J. Enterp. Inf. Manag. **30**, 320–334 (2017)
19. Nord, G., Nord, J.: Knowledge and skill requirements important for success as a system analyst. J. Inf. Technol. Manag. **6**, 47–52 (1995)
20. Aasheim, C., Li, L., Williams, S.: Knowledge and skill requirements for entry-level information technology workers: a comparison of industry and academia. J. Inf. Syst. Educ. **20**(3), 349–356 (2009)
21. Ghosh, P.: The Business Analyst in the World of Artificial Intelligence and Machine Learning, Dataversity (2017). https://www.dataversity.net/business-analyst-world-artificial-intelligence-machine-learning/. Accessed 07 Mar 2021
22. Noll, C.L., Wilkins, M.: Critical skills of is professionals: a model for curriculum development. J. Inf. Technol. Educ. **1**, 143–156 (2002)

23. Matthee, M., Turpin, M.: Teaching critical thinking, problem solving, and design thinking: preparing is students for the future. J. Inf. Syst. Educ. **30**, 242–252 (2019)
24. Kolding, M., Sundblad, M., Alexa, J., Stone, M., Aravopoulou, E., Evans, G.: Information management – a skills gap? Bottom Line (New York) **31**, 170–190 (2018)
25. Birgit, E., et al.: Smart work: the transformation of the labour market due to the fourth industrial revolution. Int. J. Bus. Econ. Sci. Appl. Res. **10**, 47–66 (2017)
26. Hahm, S.: Attitudes and performance of workers preparing for the fourth industrial revolution. KSII Trans. Internet Inf. Syst. **12**, 4038–4056 (2018)
27. Pellizzari, M., Fichen, A.: A new measure of skill mismatch: theory and evidence from PIAAC. IZA J. Labor Econ. **6**(1), 1–30 (2017). https://doi.org/10.1186/s40172-016-0051-y
28. Restrepo, P.: Skill mismatch and structural unemployment. In: MIT Job Market Paper, pp. 1–94 (2015)
29. Danaher, J.: Will life be worth living in a world without work? technological unemployment and the meaning of life. Sci. Eng. Ethics **23**(1), 41–64 (2016). https://doi.org/10.1007/s11948-016-9770-5
30. Gupta, R.: Key Business Analyst Skills Every Analyst Should Have, thebusinessanalystjobdescription.com. https://thebusinessanalystjobdescription.com/key-business-analyst-skills/. Accessed 07 Mar 2021
31. Bahirat, T.: Business Analyst Jobs 2021 Skills Required, Salary Trends and Roles (2020). https://www.mygreatlearning.com/blog/business-analyst-jobs-skills/. Accessed 07 Mar 2021
32. Hussey, D.: The New Business Analysis Ecosystem, norwalkaberdeen.com (2016). https://www.norwalkaberdeen.com/insights-2016-6. Accessed 07 Mar 2021
33. Schoeman, J.: The evolution of the business analyst – answering the why, not the what (2016). https://bsg.co.za/wp-content/uploads/2016/10/the-future-of-the-ba_bsg_business-analysts.pdf. Accessed 07 Mar 2021
34. Creswell, J.W., Plano Clark, V.L.: Designing and Conducting Mixed Methods Research. Sage, California (2017)
35. Misra, R.K., Khurana, K.: Employability skills among information technology professionals: a literature review. Procedia Comput. Sci. **113**, 63–70 (2017)
36. Zhou, K., Liu, T., Zhou, L.: Industry 4.0: towards future industrial opportunities and challenges. In: 2015 12th International Conference on Fuzzy Systems and Knowledge Discovery, pp. 2147–2152. IEEE (2015)
37. Jin, X., Wah, B.W., Cheng, X., Wang, Y.: Significance and challenges of big data research. Big Data Res. **2**(2), 59–64 (2015)
38. Harrison, Y.: Can The Business Analyst Survive The Future? BAtimes (2017). https://www.batimes.com/articles/can-the-business-analyst-survive-the-future.html. Accessed 07 Mar 2021
39. Damian, D., Helms, R., Kwan, I., Marczak, S., Koelewijn, B.: The role of domain knowledge and cross-functional communication in socio-technical coordination. In: 2013 35th International Conference on Software Engineering (ICSE), pp. 442–451 (2013)

The Impact of Role Coordination on Virtual Team Performance and Player Retention in Esports

Agnes Yang[1(✉)], De Liu[1], and Radhika Santhanam[2]

[1] Carlson School of Management, University of Minnesota, Minneapolis, MN 55455, USA
{yang6972,deliu}@umn.edu
[2] Price College of Business, University of Oklahoma, Norman, OK 73019, USA
radhika@ou.edu

Abstract. Multiplayer online battle arena games provide a valid laboratory for studying virtual-teams behavior. Despite the surging attention on virtual team collaboration, little attempts have been made to identify which factor facilitates role coordination or how role coordination affects team outcomes, although when people are collaborating virtually, coordination based on their roles can be of great help for effective teamwork. Therefore, in this first preliminary study, in our larger program of study on Role Coordination and Team Games, we examine the relationship between role coordination and team performance, player retention in highly virtual teams. Using detailed 3.59 million match data from Defense of the Ancients 2 (Dota 2), where a match-making system is engineered to encourage players to collaborate, we devise a novel measure of role coordination based on rank aggregation by the Bradley-Terry model. We report evidence that role coordination is positively associated with team performance and player retention. We further indicate that familiarity among team members facilitates role coordination. These findings have implications for the literature on virtual teams and games as well as game companies, developers, and players about how to facilitate role coordination.

Keywords: Esports · Virtual team · Role coordination · Familiarity · Competition

1 Introduction

With the diffusion of democratized digital collaboration tools (e.g., Zoom and GitHub) and remote workforces, the virtual team has played vital roles in organizations and communities ever than before. Zoom, a representative peer-to-peer video conferencing platform, recently reported that more than 300 million people are using the platform daily as of April 2020 (PRNewswire.com). Several challenges the virtual team-based platform faces are communication difficulties due to the lack of direct interaction and high need to adapt to structural changes (Gibson and Gibbs 2006). As such, the prior studies on the virtual team have primarily focused on identifying conditions under which

A. Garimella et al. (Eds.): WeB 2020, LNBIP 418, pp. 121–128, 2021.
https://doi.org/10.1007/978-3-030-79454-5_11

trust, shared understanding, and effective group interaction are enhanced (Dabbish and Kraut 2008; Gibson and Cohen 2003; Jarvenpaa et al. 1998).

However, surprisingly little attention has been paid to role coordination and an antecedent facilitating the coordination in a virtual team, though we often see cases where individuals' role selection is a key process of team composition. For instance, the Kaggle competition requires participants' judgment for which role they do fit in, such as data engineer, data science modeler, and algorithm engineer. Our research fills the gap in the current understanding of what drives virtual team coordination and aims to shed light on these research questions: Does team familiarity facilitate role coordination in the virtual context? Does role coordination drive team performance and individual engagement, respectively?

Esports, an emerging form of sport competition using multiplayer video games, provides a suitable environment to substantiate our research questions. In recent years, the popularity of Esports has risen rapidly across the globe. A recent industry report found that Esports revenues will reach $1.1 billion, and the global Esports audience will grow to 495.0 million people in 2020 (Newzoo 2020). Especially, in Defense of the Ancients 2, known as Dota 2, where the match-making system is engineered to encourage players to collaborate, the role selection process is known to be one of the determinants that lead to team success.

Our analysis indicates that teams who achieve better role coordination indeed have high performances. Importantly, role coordination also increases player retention, meaning that after experiencing successful role coordination, players will likely play the next match more quickly. We also find familiarity as an antecedent of higher role coordination.

This study makes several contributions. First, it contributes to the literature on virtual and distributed teams. Virtual teams face challenges in achieving effective team coordination. In response to these challenges, previous literature on virtual teams has studied factors that could lead to better teamwork, such as trust and shared understanding (Dabbish and Kraut 2008; Gibson and Cohen 2003). In contrast, we study a novel factor of role coordination and its antecedent, such as team familiarity. Our findings are especially important for distributed teams with short life spans and transient memberships, which are becoming more common in organizations, such as IT software development and healthcare (Vashdi et al. 2013).

Second, our work contributes to digital games literature. While previous research on games has largely focused on individual experience in games (Liu et al. 2013; Santhanam et al. 2016), we investigate in-game team dynamics and devise a novel measure of role coordination by using rich data. In doing so, we underscore the significance of the role in games where players usually do not meet each other in person.

2   Data and Method

2.1   Data

We collect a random sample of 1,000 Dota 2 matches in 3 months and augment that with past and future play history for the involved players. We firstly randomly sample 1,000 matches between April 1st and June 30th, 2019. The 1,000 matches do not include any match that meets one or more of the following exclusion criteria: 1) if any player chooses to keep their information private, 2) if any player's ranking information is missing, 3) if the party information is missing, and 4) if a non-human player is involved. For each of the 10,000 participants of these matches, we then collect play history data from January 1st to July 31st, 2019. By design, we have at least three months of play history, and at least one month of future plays for each player. We do not consider player history beyond July 2019 because a major change in Dota 2's match-making algorithm occurred on August 6, 2019. Three months of play history is reasonable because players may not recall whom she played with further back. Our dataset is drawn from both the Steam Web API and the OpenDota API.

2.2 Research Context

Dota 2 is a five-versus-five multiplayer online battle arenas (MOBAs) game. In this setting, each player must choose a hero among 119 heroes possessing different abilities including, for example, a group of "carry" heroes who specialized in offensive power, a group of "Support" heroes who keep allies alive, and a group of "Nuker" heroes who can cast high damage spells in a team fight. So, players choose whichever heroes they think is advantageous to team performance. That is, each player has options of 1) just choosing her/his favorite hero disregarding team hero combination 2) sacrificing her/his favorite hero and choosing a hero that is assumed to contribute to the team winning 3) sticking to her/his favorite hero believing that it is the best choice to the team winning. We leverage this tension as a source of role coordination and quantify it by a mixture of Bradley-Terry rank aggregation estimation and the K-means clustering approach.

2.3 Measurement

Familiarity Variable (Team-Level). Similar to Reagans et al. (2005) and Huckman et al. (2009), we measure team familiarity by first calculating, M_{ij}, the number of times each pair of team members i and j has played on the same team within the recent three months before the current match. We Aggregate This value over every unique pair on a team for our familiarity variable, defined as $\sum_{i=1}^{5} \sum_{j>i}^{5} M_{ij}$.

Role Coordination Variable (Team-Level). We construct a novel measure of role coordination by estimating the winning probability of each hero combination based on the Bradley-Terry model. The Bradley-Terry model is based on pairwise contest outcomes. The model assumes the probability of a candidate i beating j is:

$$P(i \text{ beats } j) = \frac{\gamma_i}{\gamma_i + \gamma_j}, \tag{1}$$

where γ_i is a positive-valued parameter that might be interpreted as the ability of candidate i (Hunter 2004). If the outcome of each pairwise contest between candidate i and candidate j is independent, we can aggregate model (1) to obtain the log-likelihood of the entire observed contest history between any pair of candidates:

$$\varphi(\gamma) = \sum_{i=1}^{m} \sum_{j=1}^{m} \left[w_{ij} \ln \gamma_i - w_{ij} \ln(\gamma_i + \gamma_j) \right] \tag{2}$$

where w_{ij} denotes the number of times candidate i beats candidate j. With this log-likelihood function, we can estimate parameters for all m candidates using the maximum likelihood estimation and rank the candidates $\gamma_1, \ldots, \gamma_m$ based on their relative abilities.

We cannot directly apply the Bradley-Terry model to the hero combinations because the number of distinct hero combinations of a five-player team is exceedingly large. Instead, we first perform a dimension reduction by forming a few clusters of heroes and estimation the winning chance of hero-cluster combinations (for simplicity, we still refer to it as hero combinations). Specifically, in Dota 2, heroes are characterized by 27 attributes, such as min and max damage, starting armor, and vision range. We first measure the pairwise cosine distance between all heroes over the feature space, then build a matrix for the relative distances. Next, we project the relative cosine distances onto a two-dimensional space using multidimensional scaling. Finally, we partition 119 heroes into five clusters using K-means clustering, similar to Kim et al. (2016). The choice of the number of clusters is informed by the Elbow test. Based on the result, we label the clusters as Belligerence, Agility, Intelligence, Versatility, and Supportiveness. Representative heroes for each cluster are Alchemist, Axe, Silencer, Chaos Knight, and Enigma, respectively.

By reducing 119 heroes to five representative heroes (i.e., hero clusters), we can obtain 126 hero combinations for a team of 5 players. We treat each of the 126 distinct hero combinations as a candidate in the Bradley-Terry model so that there are 7,875 (i.e., $126 \times 125/2 = 7,875$) pairs of candidates. We use the 3,596,622 historical matches played by the seed players during the sampling period to recover the "abilities" of each hero combination and use these to calculate the ability of this hero combination against the lowest-ability combination. We use this estimated ability as the hero combination's score.

To compute the role coordination score for each team, we first calculate a realized combination score then divide it by optimal combination score. The former is calculated based on the actual heroes chosen by the five players in the match. The latter is based on a hypothetical scenario that gives rise to the highest hero combination score if the five players are allowed to choose any of their top 3 most frequently-played heroes in the last three months. The latter simulates the "ideal" scenario that the team had the foresight to optimize their hero choices fully. In sum, this role coordination variable captures how well a team coordinated its roles relative to its potential optimum.

Team Performance Variable (Match-Level). The team performance variable ($Win_{i,d}$) is defined as "a dummy variable that equals one if the dire team wins a game."

Player Retention Variable (Individual-Level). The player retention variable ($PlayRetention_{ij}$) is defined as "a player retention measure calculated as the total number of minutes required for a player to reach the 5th (or 10th) game after completing a current game."

2.4 Empirical Model

To establish a relationship between team familiarity (antecedent), role coordination (mediating variable), team performance (outcome variable 1), and player retention (outcome variable 2). We estimate the following regressions models:

$$Win_{i,d} = \beta_0 + \beta_1\left(RoleCoord_{i,d} - RoleCoord_{i,r}\right) + \beta_2\left(Familiarity_{i,d} - Familiarity_{i,r}\right)$$
$$+ \beta_3\left(MMR_{i,d} - MMR_{i,r}\right) + \beta_4\left(Party_{i,d} - Party_{i,r}\right) + \beta_5 RankedMatch_i + \varepsilon_i \text{(1)}$$

$$PlayRetention_{ij} = \beta_0 + \beta_1 RoleCoord_i + \beta_2 Familiarity_i + \beta_3 MMR_j$$
$$+ \beta_4 Party_i + \beta_5 PlayFreq_j + \beta_6 RankedMatch_i + \beta_7 Win_i + \varepsilon_{ij} \text{(2)}$$

$$RoleCoord_i = \beta_0 + \beta_1 Familiarity_i + \beta_2 MMR_i + \beta_3 Party_i$$
$$+ \beta_4 RankedMatch_i + \varepsilon_i \text{(3)}$$

where *MMR* indicates average team (or individual) skill level; *Party* indicates the intensity of party-playing of each team; *PlayFreq* is a measure of play frequency calculated by the number of matches played by a focal player in the last one month; *RankedMatch* is a dummy variable that equals one if a game is a ranked match. The subscript i indicate a team; j indicates a Player; d and r indicate Dire team and Radiant team.

3 Results

First, we examine whether role coordination is associated with the winning probability in Table 1. We observe that teams with better role coordination are more likely to win the game ($\beta = 0.835$, $p < 0.05$). More specifically, one unit increase in the role coordination score is associated with an increase in the odds of winning by 0.835. The coefficient of *Familiarity* is statistically insignificant, implying that team familiarity does not directly increase the winning chance.

The following Table 1 gives a summary of all heading levels.

Table 1. Estimations on winning probability

Variables	Win
Diff_RoleCoordination	0.835**
	(0.427)
Diff_Familiarity	1.01e−05
	(0.000352)
Controls	YES
Observations	914
Pseudo r-squared	0.020

In Table 3, we examine how role coordination affects player retention. In columns (1) and (2) we show a positive relationship between role coordination and player retention

($\beta = -1,825$, p < 0.05 in column (1)). The magnitude is also economically significant in that the coefficient corresponds to about a 40.07% reduction in the minutes till the next 5th game. After experiencing high role coordination in a match, the time to take to the next games decreases. The role coordination effect is stronger when player retention is measured as the next five games than the next ten games, implying this effect diminishes as users play more games. In columns (3) and (4), we include a variable Win and still obtain significant coefficients on role coordination as in columns (1) and (2), suggesting that the variation in player retention from role coordination is not due to winning in the previous match.

As shown in Table 2, we find that an increase in team familiarity is associated with higher role coordination ($\beta = 0.0000283$, p < 0.10). There are no other significant predictors for role coordination, which may imply that the matching system of Dota 2 works as intended. When two teams are matched, the matching system is designed to equalize the skill level (i.e., MMR) and the number of party-play members between the two teams. However, the matching algorithm does not consider familiarity, and thus variations in familiarity work as an exogenous shock.

Table 2. Estimations on role coordination

Variables	Role coordination
Familiarity	2.83e−05*
	(1.51e−05)
Controls	YES
Observations	1,828
R-squared	0.002

Table 3. Estimations on player retention

Variables	Time2Next 5Game	Time2Next 10Game	Time2Next 5Game	Time2Next 10Game
Role coordination	−1,825**	−2,210*	−1,741**	−2,113*
	(847.4)	(1,174)	(851.9)	(1,179)
Familiarity	−0.504	−0.500	−0.580	−0.579
	(1.264)	(1.981)	(1.275)	(2.004)
Win			−419.2**	−501.2**
			(167.6)	(238.7)
Controls	YES	YES	YES	YES
Observations	9,395	9,304	9,395	9,304
R-squared	0.074	0.113	0.075	0.114

Robust standard errors in parentheses. *, **, and *** represent significance at the 10%, 5%, and 1% level, respectively (same for all the tables).

4 Conclusion

The primary goal of this study is to examine how role coordination in virtual teams affects team performance and member retention, and what leads to better role coordination. We explore these questions in the context of team-based Esports games, using a unique and large data set obtained from the popular online game Dota 2. Our results suggest that team familiarity leads to better role coordination, which, in turn, causes improvements in team performance and member retention.

Overall, the results suggest that role coordination plays a key role in winning probability and in player retention. Also, we find an antecedent of role coordination, team familiarity. While several prior studies report the direct positive impact of team familiarity on team performance, our results highlight the intermediate role of role coordination between team familiarity and performance.

Our analysis indicates that teams who achieve better role coordination indeed have high performances. Importantly, role coordination also increases player retention, meaning that after experiencing successful role coordination, players will likely play the next match more quickly. We also find familiarity as an antecedent of higher role coordination.

The findings of this study have practical implications for game companies and developers. Knowing the importance of role coordination allows game companies and developers to devise enhanced match-making algorithms that lead to better role coordination and improved game experience. For example, Esports platforms could adjust their matching algorithm by matching players with familiar teammates if possible. Additionally, they may help teams coordinate roles better by making hero recommendations. Our study also contributes to the literature on virtual teams in organizations and digital games by introducing a novel concept and measurement of role coordination.

References

Dabbish, L., Kraut, R.: Research note—awareness displays and social motivation for coordinating communication. Inf. Syst. Res. **19**(2), 221–238 (2008)

Gibson, C.B., Cohen, S.G. (eds.): Virtual Teams that Work: Creating Conditions for Virtual Team Effectiveness. John Wiley & Sons, Hoboken (2003)

Gibson, C.B., Gibbs, J.L.: Unpacking the concept of virtuality: the effects of geographic dispersion, electronic dependence, dynamic structure, and national diversity on team innovation. Adm. Sci. Q. **51**(3), 451–495 (2006)

Huckman, R.S., Staats, B.R., Upton, D.M.: Team familiarity, role experience, and performance: evidence from Indian software services. Manage. Sci. **55**(1), 85–100 (2009)

Hunter, D.R.: MM algorithms for generalized Bradley-Terry models. Ann. Stat. **32**(1), 384–406 (2004)

Jarvenpaa, S., Shaw, T.R.: Global virtual teams: integrating models of trust. In: Sieber, P., Griese, J. (eds.) Organizational Virtualness. Proceedings of the VoNet -Workshop, pp. 35–52 Simowa-Verlag, Bern (1998)

Kim, J., Keegan, B.C., Park, S., Oh, A.: The proficiency-congruency dilemma: virtual team design and performance in multiplayer online games. In: Proceedings of the 2016 CHI Conference on Human Factors in Computing Systems, pp. 4351–4365 (2016)

Liu, D., Li, X., Santhanam, R.: Digital games and beyond: what happens when players compete? MIS Q. **37**, 111–124 (2013)

Newzoo. Global Esports Market Report 2020 (2020). https://newzoo.com/insights/trend-reports/
newzoo-global-esports-market-report-2020-light-version/#:~:text=Highlights%3A,from%
20media%20rights%20&%20sponsorship. Accessed 07 Mar 2021

Reagans, R., Argote, L., Brooks, D.: Individual experience and experience working together:
predicting learning rates from knowing who knows what and knowing how to work together.
Manage. Sci. **51**(6), 869–881 (2005)

Santhanam, R., Liu, D., Shen, W.C.M.: Research Note—Gamification of technology-mediated
training: not all competitions are the same. Inf. Syst. Res. **27**(2), 453–465 (2016)

Vashdi, D.R., Bamberger, P.A., Erez, M.: Can surgical teams ever learn? The role of coordination,
complexity, and transitivity in action team learning. Acad. Manag. J. **56**(4), 945–971 (2013)

An Analysis of Characteristics Affecting Trust Formation in Human Versus Machine Interactions from a Systematic Literature Review Perspective

M A Shariful Amin[✉] and Dan J. Kim[✉]

University of North Texas, Denton, TX 76203, USA
{mashariful.amin,dan.kim}@unt.edu

Abstract. This study aims to identify characteristics affecting trust in human versus machine interactions through a systematic literature review (SLR) of articles about trust in machine/object. We perform a systematic literature search focusing on trust in humans and trust in machines, identify a total of 85 relevant studies, and find two sets of focal dimensions of trust in object/machine. The first set of dimensions are related to the trust in human characteristics such as benevolence, ability, the integrity of object/machine, and the second set of characteristics are related to trust in mechanical/machine characteristics like performance, integrity, purpose, and structural assurance/organizational factors. The results of SLR indicate the evolution of trust and the dynamic relationship between trustor and trustee in terms of the trustor's disposition/culture, privacy and security. The study also discusses the dynamic trust relationship between trustor and trustee and how over trust and distrust impact the relationship between trustor and trustee.

Keywords: Trust · Trust in human versus machine characteristics · Information technology (IT) · Trustor-trustee · Human-machine interaction (HMI) · Dynamic trust relationships · Information systems (IS)

1 Introduction

For the last couple of decades, trust has been presented as an all-powerful lubricant [1] that keeps the world's economic wheels turning and greases the right connections [2]. Muir and Moray [3] extended a model of trust between people, to establish trust between humans and machines. They argued that the concept of trust is essentially necessary as humans can never completely encompass the internal mechanisms of automated systems. In the 21st century, technology has become readily accessible and affordable to users [4]. The expansion of technology advancements such as the internet, websites, mobile devices, robots, especially artificial intelligence (AI), e-Health and e-commerce has advanced our everyday life [5].

Intelligent systems such as mobile devices, algorithms and machines known as artificial intelligence (AI) have become more common in everyone's daily lives. With the

© Springer Nature Switzerland AG 2021
A. Garimella et al. (Eds.): WeB 2020, LNBIP 418, pp. 129–136, 2021.
https://doi.org/10.1007/978-3-030-79454-5_12

advancement in technology such as information technology (IT), human interaction with intelligent systems/machines is rapidly increasing [6]. Hence, establishing trust between humans and machine is an upcoming challenge to overcome. While many researchers and organizations are progressing towards a technology-enabled society, there are still problems in the way humans trust technology. For example, the fear of being spied on is still prevailing, resulting in people covering their webcams. Many people are still worried that organizations like Cambridge Analytica are leaking their data [7].

This study aims to identify the factors that a trustor (human) looks for in a trustee (object/machine) to form trust and evaluate how this trust evolves between the trustors and trustees. Trust is a conceptual model based on the characteristics of the trustee such as intentions, beliefs, and behaviour [8–10]. The purpose of this paper is to offer a thorough review of the trustor developing trust in machines such as artificial intelligence (AI), mobile devices, and addressing prior contradictory studies. Trust in all partnerships is a crucial foundations variable; it is even more important when it comes to understanding the collaboration between humans and technology such as a robot or artificial intelligence. Just as trust mediates human relationships, it could also mediate human-machine relationships [11].

2 Theoretical Background of Trust

Trust and Rationality: The emotional bond is not just about the relationship but is also the trust in the trustee's character and integrity or "benevolence" in the relationship of trust with the trustor. Most of the information system re- searchers [12] or trust scholars still adopt this strategy, focusing on the most used and recognized concept of trust. As per Mayer et al. [9], trust is the willingness of an individual, the trustor is described as a person who is willing to be vulnerable to the actions of another individual or entity, and the trustee waits based on the expectation that the other will perform a particular action important to the trustor, irrespective of the ability to monitor or control that other party [13, 14]. Mayer's definition and other concepts used in Information Systems (IS) literature have their origins in the philosophy of management and focus on the trust between individuals, groups of people, or organizations [15]. Since early trust studies have concentrated on research using this trust relationship, most authors have implemented three dimensions of trustworthiness–ability, benevolence, and integrity by Mayer et al. [9] to measure trust between two entities [16]. Likewise, in their article, Hoff and Bashir [17] note that socially learned principles, such as politeness, were extended in the 1990s to machine interactions and how one perceives trust in the machine [17–19]. Interpersonal trust is initially based on the mere predictability of a trustee's actions because people tend to enter relationships with strangers cautiously. The trustee's dependability or integrity becomes the central foundation as interpersonal trust develops [20]. Finally, fully developed interpersonal trust is grounded on faith or benevolence; therefore, the human-machine trust often developments in the reverse order. Research suggests that people are often favourably biased when trusting new machines or technologies [17, 21]. Machines are generally believed to be flawless. However, their initial trust disappears following system errors.

Human Trust: Trust arises when the trustor develops faith in the trustee's capability of truthfulness to forecast its future actions. Therefore, a conceptual hypothesis essential to the building of the trust process is that human behaviour is generally consistent and predictable [22]. Trust is established when an inter-personal bond of promise and expectation is created between people, allowing them to move beyond logical prediction to take a "leap of faith" that trust will be maintained [15, 23].

Machine Trust: Human trust is not necessarily the same as human and machine trust or trust between artificial intelligence as per Singh and Sirdeshmukh [24]. Trust arises when the trustor develops faith in the trustee's capability of truthfulness to forecast its future actions. Researchers use the dimensions laid out by Lee and Moray [25] to assess the trust between humans and machines: performance, process, and purpose. Performance represents the machine's ability to help people achieve their goals. The process demonstrates the perception of the user to the extent to which the algorithms and processes of the machine are suitable. Purpose represents the understanding of the human user's intention of the machine developer's expectations and their expectation of the future value of using artificial intelligence, robot, or machine. The purpose of our research is to study the dynamic relationship between trustor and trustee by questioning the factors trustor (human) look in the trustee (object/machine) to form trust and trying to find out how trust evolves between the trustor and trustees.

3 Research Methodology

Search Query: Search strings are primarily defined on June 2020, the Web of Science, the IEEE Digital Library (Xplore), ACM digital library, and Association for Information Systems (AIS) e-Library Databases were searched by breaking down each question into individual facets and selecting the most competitive keywords concerning this subject. After variant steps of utilizing a list of synonyms and alternative spelling considering subject headings used in journals and databases during initial analysis other terms were obtained. The search string was constructed by examining the coverage of outcomes by associating the Boolean operator AND, Boolean operator OR of the primary search. Hence, three keywords "Trust", "Trust in human", and "Trust in the machine" was selected. The specified technology evaluation string was (Trust* AND (machine OR website OR Robot OR "smart device")) and (Trust* AND (human OR people OR person OR individual)) (See Table 1). In the preliminary stage, the aforementioned string was applied to the title of articles, keywords of articles, and abstract of articles then it was integrated with the Boolean operator AND to accentuate the lack of comprehensive investigation and technical comparison on existing approaches up to now. Further, the Boolean operator OR was used to broaden the search by connecting the output obtained in the previous step. We conducted this research in June 2020 and specified a time range from 2010 to the end of May 2020. Table 2 shows the number of relevant articles analyzed (n = 85) SLR process.

To sum it up, Fig. 1 shows that, those articles that contained inadequate terms or were not conclusive, not fitting search terms, not related to the research topic, not having quality evaluation, no description, or no specification of terms were removed. We are

Table 1. Search keywords used for human versus machine trust in the SLR

Human trust	VS.	Machine trust	Databases	Fields
"Trust in" AND (Human OR People OR Person OR Individual)		"Trust in" AND (Machine OR Website OR Robot OR "Smart Devices" OR "Technology" OR "Artificial Intelligent*)"	Web of Sciences (WoS)	Title, Keywords, Abstract, Other-Relevant Articles
			ACM Digital Library	
			IEEE Explore	
			AIS Electronic Library	

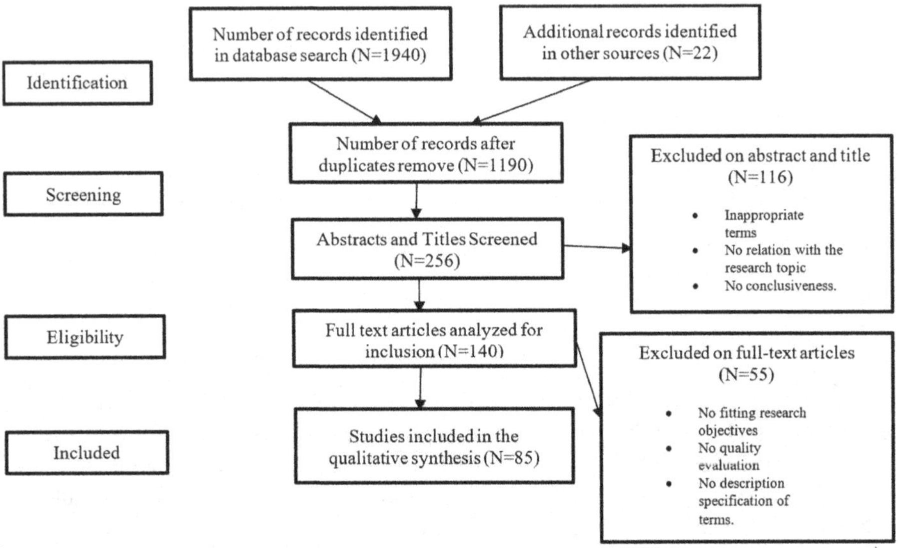

Fig. 1. Selection of relevant articles in the SLR process

presenting our systematic literature review (SLR) process based on the PRISMA diagram by Moher et al. [26]. The process flow chart/diagram that shows each of the steps carried out for the development of the SLR is presented.

4   Results and Discussion

Based on a concept-centric analysis of 85 identified papers as listed in Fig. 1, we were able to identify two main research perspectives. It was observed that there are two dimensions of trust in an object or machine. The first dimension is trust in perceived human characteristics of object/machine and the second dimension is trust in the perceived machine or mechanical characteristics of trust. Furthermore, trustor's disposition in culture, privacy, security, and environment [27] determines their trust in trustees (object/machine). The

Table 2. Preliminary analysis and results of SLR process

DataBase	Initial search results	Number of relevant articles (Either of the relevant words are present)	Final number of relevant articles
Web of Sciences	736	530	29
The IEEE Digital Library	85	44	16
ACM Digital Library	449	314	20
AIS Electronic Library	648	289	12
Google Scholar (internet-based)	22	13	08
Total	**1,940**	**1,190**	**85**

initial trust develops between trustor and trustee through the first few interactions as interaction increases, the trust starts building up and then reach a level where trustor and trustee work in harmony. Based on our findings, the trustor sometimes starts over trusting the trustee which may lead to erroneous decision making.

Trust in Perceived Human Characteristics of Machine/Object: Treating an agent as human versus non-human (machine) has a powerful impact on whether those agents are treated as agents worthy of trust or just as an object. There are two dimensions of treating non-human agent/object as human. The first dimension involves attributing humanlike physical features to non-humans (shape, a face, and hands), and the second dimension involves attributing hu-manlike soft character to nonhumans such as benevolence, ability, and integrity [28]. In our SLR we found that the soft character of humans in non-humans plays a key role in forming trust in the trustor.

Trust in Perceived Machine Characteristics of Object/Machine: Based on the capability and skill of the system, If the machine can achieve the necessary goals, then the trust will be established. As Lee et al., and Hancock et al. discussed in their research, the performance of the machine promotes trustors trust [29, 30]. The result of studies conducted by Vogiatzis and Karkaletsis [31] and Lankton and McKnight [32] has shown that reliability and trust plays a vital role in robot-to-robot(machine) team, and constructed cognitive model comprised of modules - reactive, deliberative, reflective, and effective to understand the reliability of trustor.

5 Trustor Characteristics

Common factors influencing trustees/human's trust in trustors/machines include disposition of culture, privacy and security, distrust, and over-trust [33]. The personal and impersonal sources of information had different impacts on individuals across cultures according to Dawar et al. [34]. Privacy was found to be a key concern that affects trust-building in machine/chatbots [35]. As per the research of Yang et al. [36] a higher level of Artificial Intelligent transparency may mitigate privacy concern and build trust between trustor and trustee [27]. Furthermore, Inagaki and Itoh [37] defined over-trust as an incorrect situation of a diagnostic decision where the user believes that the object is trustworthy although it is not trustworthy [37]. It was stated by Dong in 2015 [38] that sometimes people trust too much in the decision-making capabilities of these systems. This propensity of overtrust in object/machine related to high-risk activities, such as in healthcare is concerning. As per the research of Baker et al. [39], when the machine fails to perform as per expectation then a violation of trust occurs, and to win back trust trustee needs to repair the broken trust.

6 Expected Contributions

We applied the SLR approach to examine the establishment of trust between trustor and trustee which can be studied further. Future holds a lot of scopes to analyze the trust characteristics based on the trustor's attributes and trustee/object/machine attributes. Furthermore, the trustor's characteristics - disposition, culture, and privacy risk also affect the trust formation between trustor and trustee [40]. The result of SLR has theoretical implications for future research. Our results showed that with the advancement of technology, there is a growing need for the formation of trust between humans and machines. Researchers should start creating literature based on the trust formation between humans and machines, with a particular focus on security and privacy [41]. The identified relationship must be studied in-depth, as well as put to the test by human-machine interaction (HMI) experts, engineers, and information science as well as information systems experts to ensure that trust formation is understood in depth between humans and machines [42].

The application of proper functioning between human-machine interaction such as artificial intelligence trust [43] will be beneficial for future research and implementation.

References

1. Zak, P.: Trust factor: the science of creating high-performance companies. Amacom.com
2. Kramer, A.D., Guillory, J.E., Hancock, J.T.: Experimental evidence of massive-scale emotional contagion through social networks. Proc. Natl. Acad. Sci. **111**(24), 8788–8790 (2014)
3. Muir, B.M., Moray, N.: Trust in automation. Part II. Experimental studies of trust and human intervention in a process control simulation. Ergonomics **39**(3), 429–460 (1996)
4. Robin, B.R.: Digital storytelling: a powerful technology tool for the 21st century classroom. Theory Pract. **47**(3), 220–228 (2008)
5. Yun, H., Lee, G., Kim, D.J.: A chronological review of empirical research on personal information privacy concerns: an analysis of contexts and research con- structs. Inf. Manage. **56**(4), 570–601 (2019). https://doi.org/10.1016/j.im.2018.10.001
6. Hsu, K.K.: Discussion on the live broadcast of social media and e-commerce (2019)
7. Angelopoulos, S., Brown, M., McAuley, D., Merali, Y., Mortier, R., Price, D.: Stewardship of personal data on social networking sites. Int. J. Inf. Manage. **56**, 102208 (2020)

8. Bhattacharya, R., Devinney, T.M., Pillutla, M.M.: A formal model of trust based on outcomes. Acad. Manag. Rev. **23**(3), 459–472 (1998)
9. Mayer, R.C., Davis, J.H., Schoorman, F.D.: An integrative model of organizational trust. Acad. Manag. Rev. **20**(3), 709–734 (1995)
10. Ross, W., LaCroix, J.: Multiple meanings of trust in negotiation theory and research: a literature review and integrative model. Int. J. Confl. Manag. **7** (1996)
11. Rotter, J.B.: A new scale for the measurement of interpersonal trust. J. Pers. **35**, 651–665 (1967)
12. Tung, F.C., Chang, S.C., Chou, C.M.: An extension of trust and TAM model with IDT in the adoption of the electronic logistics information system in HIS in the medical industry. Int. J. Med. Informatics **77**(5), 324–335 (2008)
13. Rousseau, D.M., Sitkin, S.B., Burt, R.S., Camerer, C.: Not so different at all: a cross disziplinary view of trust. Acad. Manag. Rev. **23**(3), 393–404 (1998)
14. Ssllner, M., Pavlou, P.A., Leimeister, J.M.: Understanding trust in IT artifacts a new conceptual approach. SSRN Electron. J. (2013). https://doi.org/10.2139/ssrn.2475382
15. Lee, J.D., See, K.A.: Trust in automation: designing for appropriate reliance. Hum. Fact. J. Hum. Fact. Ergon. Soc. **46**(1), 50–80 (2004). https://doi.org/10.1518/hfes.46.1.50.30392
16. McKnight, D.H., Choudhury, V., Kacmar, C.: Developing and validating trust measures for e-commerce: an integrative typology. Inf. Syst. Res. **13**(3), 334–359 (2002)
17. Hoff, K.A., Bashir, M.: Trust in automation: integrating empirical evidence on factors that influence trust. Hum. Factors **57**(3), 407–434 (2015)
18. Nass, C., Moon, Y., Carney, P.: Are people polite to computers? Responses to computer-based interviewing systems 1. J. Appl. Soc. Psychol. **29**(5), 1093–1109 (1999)
19. Nass, C., Steuer, J., Tauber, E.R.: Computers are social actors. In: Proceedings of the SIGCHI Conference on Human Factors in Computing Systems, pp. 72–78, April 1994
20. Riedl, R., Hubert, M., Kenning, P.: Are there neural gender differences in online trust? An fMRI study on the perceived trustworthiness of eBay offers. MIS Q. **34**(2), 397–428 (2010)
21. Dzindolet, M.T., Peterson, S.A., Pomranky, R.A., Pierce, L.G., Beck, H.P.: The role of trust in automation reliance. Int. J. Hum. Comput. Stud. **58**(6), 697–718 (2003)
22. Doney, P.M., Cannon, J.P., Mullen, M.R.: Understanding the influence of national culture on the development of trust. Acad. Manag. Rev. **23**(3), 601–620 (1998)
23. Lewis, J.D., Weigert, A.J.: Social atomism, holism, and trust. Sociol. Q. **26**(4), 455–471 (1985)
24. Singh, J., Sirdeshmukh, D.: Agency and trust mechanisms in consumer satisfaction and loyalty judgments. J. Acad. Mark. Sci. **28**(1), 150–167 (2000)
25. Lee, J., Moray, N.: Trust, control strategies and allocation of function in human-machine systems. Ergonomics **35**(10), 1243–1270 (1992)
26. Moher, D., Liberati, A., Tetzlaff, J., Altman, D.G., Prisma Group: Preferred reporting items for systematic reviews and meta-analyses: the PRISMA statement. PLoS Med. **6**(7), e1000097 (2009)
27. Lui, A., Lamb, G.W.: Artificial intelligence and augmented intelligence collaboration: regaining trust and confidence in the financial sector. Inf. Commun. Technol. Law **27**(3), 267–283 (2018)
28. Lesher, J.H.: Xenophanes of Kolophon. The Encyclopedia of Ancient History, pp. 1–2 (2013)
29. Hancock, P.A., Billings, D.R., Schaefer, K.E., Chen, J.Y., De Visser, E.J., Parasuraman, R.: A meta-analysis of factors affecting trust in human-robot interaction. Hum. Factors **53**(5), 517–527 (2011)
30. Lee, J., Park, D.H., Han, I.: The different effects of online consumer reviews on consumers' purchase intentions depending on trust in online shopping malls: an advertising perspective. Internet research (2011)

31. Vogiatzis, D., Karkaletsis, V.: A cognitive framework for robot guides in art collections. Univ. Access Inf. Soc. **10**(2), 179–193 (2011)

32. Lankton, N.K., McKnight, D.H.: What does it mean to trust facebook? Examining technology and interpersonal trust beliefs. ACM SIGMIS Database DATABASE Adv. Inf. Syst. **42**(2), 32–54 (2011)

33. Wang, S.W., Ngamsiriudom, W., Hsieh, C.H.: Trust disposition, trust antecedents, trust, and behavioral intention. Serv. Ind. J. **35**(10), 555–572 (2015)

34. Dawar, N., Parker, P.M., Price, L.J.: A cross-cultural study of interper-sonal information exchange. J. Int. Bus. Stud. **27**(3), 497–516 (1996)

35. Wang, Y., Humphrey, L.R., Liao, Z., Zheng, H.: Trust-based multi-robot symbolic motion planning with a human-in-the-loop. ACM Trans. Interactive Intell. Syst. (TiiS) **8**(4), 1–33 (2018)

36. Yang, X.J., Unhelkar, V.V., Li, K., Shah, J.A.: Evaluating effects of user experience and system transparency on trust in automation. In: 2017 12th ACM/IEEE International Conference on Human-Robot Interaction HRI, pp. 408– 416. IEEE, March 2017

37. Inagaki, T., Itoh, M.: Humans over trust in and overreliance on advanced driver assistance systems: a theoretical framework. Int. J. Veh. Technol. **2013** (2013)

38. Dong, X.L., Srivastava, D.: Big data integration. Synth. Lect. Data Manage. **7**(1), 1–198 (2015)

39. Baker, A.L., Phillips, E.K., Ullman, D., Keebler, J.R.: Toward an understanding of trust repair in human-robot interaction: current research and future directions. ACM Trans. Inter. Intell. Syst. (TiiS) **8**(4), 1–30 (2018)

40. Roy, S.K., Kesharwani, A., Bisht, S.S.: The impact of trust and perceived risk on internet banking adoption in India. Int. J. Bank Market. (2012)

41. Aroyo, A.M., Rea, F., Sandini, G., Sciutti, A.: Trust and social engineering in human robot interaction: will a robot make you disclose sensitive information, conform to its recommendations or gamble? IEEE Robot. Autom. Lett. **3**(4), 3701–3708 (2018)

42. Ekman, F., Johansson, M., Sochor, J.: Creating appropriate trust in automated vehicle systems: a framework for HMI design. IEEE Trans. Hum. Mach. Syst. **48**(1), 95–101 (2017)

43. Schmidt, P., Biessmann, F., Teubner, T.: Transparency and trust in artificial intelligence systems. J. Decis. Syst. **29**, 1–19 (2020)

Author Index

Printed in the United States
by Baker & Taylor Publisher Services